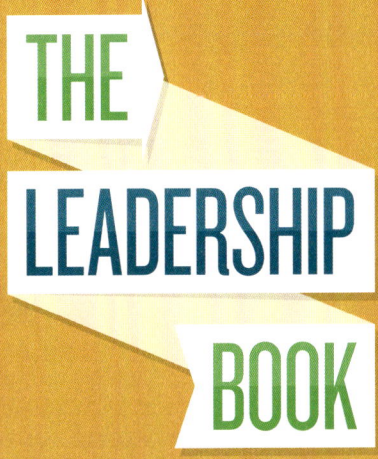

THE LEADERSHIP BOOK

by Neil Jurd

About Neil Jurd

Neil Jurd has been leading others or working in leadership development for most of his working life. As an officer in the British Army, he served in Iraq, Yemen, Bosnia and Sierra Leone, as well as teaching leadership at the Royal Military Academy Sandhurst, sitting on the Army Officer Selection Board, and graduating from Advanced Command and Staff College. He was injured by enemy mortar fire leading his Gurkha Squadron in Iraq, and was commended for leadership as a junior officer.

Since leaving the Army in 2009, he has become one of the UK's top names in leadership development, working with the Leadership Trust, Commonwealth Games Team Scotland and the NHS. Recently he captured his ideas on leadership and team development in a series of 30 videos which are available on his website, neiljurd.com.

Neil is the National Director of Initial Officer Training for the Army Cadet Force, and in 2020 was awarded a British Citizen Award for his own leadership in the voluntary sector. Neil has an MA from Cranfield University, studied Strategy at Manchester Business School and is a Fellow of both the Institute of Leadership and Management, and the Institute of Logistics and Transport. Neil lives in the Lake District, in Northern England, with his partner Macarena and their children.

CONTENTS

INTRODUCTION   10

HOW TO USE THIS BOOK   11

AUTHOR'S NOTE   11

Part One – Leadership

1.1	What is Leadership?	16
1.2	Management and Leadership – Striking the Balance	19
1.3	Asymmetric Leadership	22
1.4	The Need for a Clear and Compelling Purpose	26
1.5	Leading with Humility	30
1.6	False Leadership	32
1.7	Universal Leadership Behaviours	33
1.8	Leadership Behaviour – The Need to Clear Space	36
1.9	Different Leadership Styles	38
1.10	Keeping Leadership Positive – Leading in the Blue Zone	43

Part Two – People

2.1	Self-Knowledge and Self-Control	50
2.2	The Merril and Reid Social Styles Model	52
2.3	Some Ways to Get to Know Yourself	57
2.4	Understanding Different Perspectives	59
2.5	The Smartphone Analogy	61
2.6	Finding Out What Others are Thinking	62
2.7	Connecting with People	64
2.8	Relationships, Trust and Mutual Understanding	67
2.9	Levels of Communication	71
2.10	Developmental Conversations	75
2.11	Developing Others – Coaching as a Leader	83
2.12	Developing Others – The Performance Equation	90
2.13	Understanding Yourself – Input, Process and Output	95
2.14	Understanding People – The Foundations Model	98

Part Three – Leading Teams and Organisations

3.1	Define and Share your Style and Vision Early	101
3.2	Mission Command – Why Napoleon Did Not Meddle	104
3.3	The Importance of Diversity and Inclusion	109
3.4	Focusing Effort	112
3.5	Making Decisions - The OODA Loop	116
3.6	Building a Great Team – From Stagnation to Excellence	119
3.7	Reducing Friction – The Team Routine Service	124
3.8	Getting Your Message Though - Barriers to Communication	127
3.9	PLC – 3 Components of Success	131

Part Four – Final Words   134

INTRODUCTION

I have written this book to encourage and enable effective leadership. Leadership is a simple but powerful concept which anyone with an open mind can apply: it is about knowing where you are going and recruiting others to help.

I know that leadership can be learned, and that anyone who chooses to work to improve their leadership will be able to do so. Better leadership means happier teams, and better output. And on a greater scale, better leadership means a better world.

This book will help.

HOW TO USE THIS BOOK

I suggest you take it slowly; read a section, think about it, and see if you can apply the learning. You might find it takes you weeks or even months to work your way through the book. If that is the case and if you apply the lessons and ideas as you go, it will have been time well spent.

If you lead or are part of a team, you might share the ideas in this book with the rest of the team and think about how they apply in your context. If you have a coach, then you might explore these ideas in your coaching. Throughout the book you will find exercises and coaching questions designed to help focus your thinking and provoke positive change.

Leading well will significantly increase your positive effect in the world. Thank you for choosing this book and good luck with developing your leadership.

AUTHOR'S NOTE

This book is not intended as an academic work: the original concept was just to capture ideas that I use in my coaching and team development work. Where I have used, or knowingly been influenced by other people's ideas, I have referenced them. I have used consistent terminology throughout this book, and in most cases have retrospectively applied this consistent terminology on the models I describe. I have done this so that the reader can more easily follow the simple ideas that run though this book, without being distracted by different terms for similar ideas.

I have always felt that this prayer says something important.
For me, it is a mandate to make the world a better place.
I hope this book will help the reader to change the things
which should be changed.

SERENITY PRAYER

God, give me grace to accept with serenity the things that cannot be changed, Courage to change the things which should be changed, and the Wisdom to distinguish the one from the other.

Part One **Leadership**

PART ONE

LEADERSHIP

THIS SECTION WILL HELP YOU UNDERSTAND WHAT EFFECTIVE LEADERSHIP IS AND HOW IT DIFFERS FROM MANAGEMENT

Part One **Leadership**

1.1 What is Leadership?

A great way to 'ground' everything that follows is to start by being clear what leadership is. Often when I ask people to think about what they think leadership is, the answers are clearly inspired by internet *memes* which add more volume than value to the discussion.

Leadership isn't complicated, and I think it is useful to be clear about that. Effective leadership can be learned and developed, and it doesn't require a huge amount of study. There is a link throughout this book to the concept of teams, because effective leaders usually build strong and empowered teams.

I will start with my own clear and simple definition of leadership, which is a thread through my work.

"Leaders achieve things far beyond what they could do alone, by engaging others intellectually and emotionally in pursuit of a clear and compelling purpose." [1]

This definition is simple and straightforward and to cut to the conclusion, if you can bring that definition to life, you'll be having a positive leadership effect. This book will help you to make that happen.

I'm going to break that definition down into smaller parts, and then expand on them, to help you understand it. First **'Leaders achieve things far beyond what they could do alone...'**, leadership has reach because it creates and harnesses energy in others. An effective leader multiplies their own effect by the number of people they lead.

The Leadership Book by Neil Jurd

"Leaders achieve things far beyond what they could do alone, by engaging others intellectually and emotionally in pursuit of a clear and compelling purpose."[1]

NJ

Looking back to the definition, the leader does this *"...by engaging others intellectually and emotionally'.* Effective leaders connect with people at both levels; an emotional connection is essential to create energy and commitment. People are more likely to give time and effort to something or someone they feel an emotional connection to. Later in this book I write more about the importance of a leader taking time to get to know people and I suggest ways of achieving this, but I will mention now that position and status are barriers to building strong connections, and effective leaders work hard to make others feel comfortable. When Field Marshall Lord William Slim told cadets in Sandhurst in the 1960s that 'Leadership is just plain you'[2], he meant that their personality was a far more useful leadership tool than the rank they would hold.

But emotional engagement alone does not make for effective leadership; intellectual engagement is also important, and elements of this would include a good plan, structure, and order. Often in strong leadership partnerships one leader will prefer emotional connection, and another will be more comfortable with the intellectual: thus the two balance each other effectively and the needs of the organisation are met.

And the definition ends with the need for the leaders to focus effort *'in pursuit of a clear and compelling purpose'.* Where the purpose is not clear, activity is unfocussed. Where the purpose is not compelling there is a lack of energy and engagement. When the purpose is both clear and compelling this supplies a powerful motivator, which gives direction and inspires creativity and useful initiative.

You will read more about these ideas as you go through this book. Hopefully though, you will be getting the feeling that leadership is not hard, and that there are some simple things you can focus on already which will allow you to nurture and grow your own leadership skills.

Reflection

Look back at the definition of a leader.

- *If you were to apply that definition to your own leadership, what changes would the people that you lead see?*

1.2 Management and Leadership – Striking the Balance

Early on in this book it is worth covering the difference between leadership and management. This is a classic first morning session on most leadership courses and I usually spend half of it gently batting away more Facebook wisdom. The terms leadership and management are often used to mean the same thing, but they really don't. Organisations often have 'senior leadership teams' but putting the word leadership in the group title isn't enough to make leadership happen; leadership is a series of actions and behaviours, not just a title.

In my definition of leadership, I talk about leaders achieving more than they could alone by engaging others, and that is where the difference lies: leadership is about people. Leaders must understand, connect with, and inspire people. And people will achieve more when they are well-led. Leaders bring out the best in people.

But organisations are not just about people. They have resources such as money, vehicles, buildings and time. With these things there will be procedures to follow, inspections to pass and accounts to file. Resources can be unforgiving; it isn't possible to inspire a vehicle to pass its annual safety inspection. Resources need to be well managed.

In my experience, the difference between leadership and management is clear. Leadership is about people, and management applies to resources. In an effective organisation the two things come together, with well-led people managing resources effectively.

And striking the right balance right between leadership and management is important.

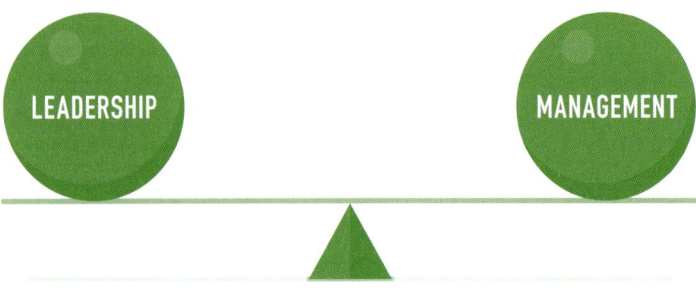

Fig.1 Illustration showing leadership and management balance.

Effective management makes people feel safe. They know their equipment is well-maintained, and they will be paid on time. Effective leadership inspires them to do more: to create, to innovate, to work a little harder. But sometimes the balance between leadership and management isn't right. Management can be too weak or too strong.

Where management is too weak, things become chaotic and the organisation carries unnecessary risk. Where management is too strong, process is much more important than purpose. People feel disempowered and disconnected and decision-making is slow and bureaucratic.

But when Management is 'just right' it provides the structure within which leadership can flourish throughout the organisation.

You might liken this to a Space Shuttle Mission (no, this isn't the story about the cleaner helping put a man on the moon). The director of NASA is only able to achieve that leadership objective of putting a crew into space because of the sound management that goes on behind the scenes. That includes the accountants making the budget balance, the logisticians making sure that the food has enough calories, and the engineers who carry out routine maintenance on the rockets. And, I suppose the cleaner – but this wasn't about him.

In effective organisations, leadership and management are both essential components of success. Management creates the conditions for success, and leadership engages and inspires the people. For sustained high-performance, you need both.

Exercise
Can you list any changes you would make in your own environment to improve the balance between Leadership and Management? - (Even if you are not empowered to make these changes, listing them is a useful thinking exercise).

1.

2.

3.

Leadership Partnerships
Some people lean towards inspiring people and emotional connection, others prefer planning and managing resources. Many successful people balance their own preferences with a deputy, or team members whose different preferences complement their own behaviours. A 'people person' might work closely with a 'detail person'. This is one reason diversity in teams is so important; effective leaders need people who offer different skills and ways of thinking from their own. I've always been an ideas and people person. In a previous role I was lucky to have a deputy who loved detail and plans. We saw the world differently but worked together effectively.

1.3 Asymmetric Leadership

Anyone can lead. In high-performing organisations this is exactly what happens: leadership flows around and throughout. Everybody is motivated and guided by that magical clear and compelling purpose, and the result is a creative and exciting culture, where leadership is encouraged and team members feel free to harness the energy of others to generate useful activity. I call this 'asymmetric leadership'.

However high-performing organisations are rare. Very often process becomes more important than Purpose, and organisations tie themselves up with bureaucracy that actually discourages initiative and leadership. Senior members of the organisation control everything, and energy is stifled. I expand on this theme in Chapter 3.6, where I introduce the 'Stagnation to Excellence' model. You might want to flick ahead and have a look at that now. In short, 'Stagnant' organisations have strict control of all activity, discourage initiative, and are strictly hierarchical.

This means that there is a very traditional view of leadership, where leadership is linked to position, grade and status. Decisions flow downhill, and nothing happens without the right level or authority signing up to it. There is an implicit (and nonsensical) assumption that with position comes immense wisdom and infallibility. You might like to see if you can list a few infallible leaders from history and think about how well things worked out for the people they led. Normally the result of this style of one-directional leadership is that decision-making is slow, and thinking is limited to only a very few authorised senior staff.

If the purpose is clear and well-understood, any member of the team can bring others together to work towards it. This could mean leading people of the same grade by harnessing their energy and getting them emotionally and intellectually engaged, or it could mean leading people of a higher grade. The illustration on the next page captures how I envision leadership flowing up, down and around in a vibrant organisation.

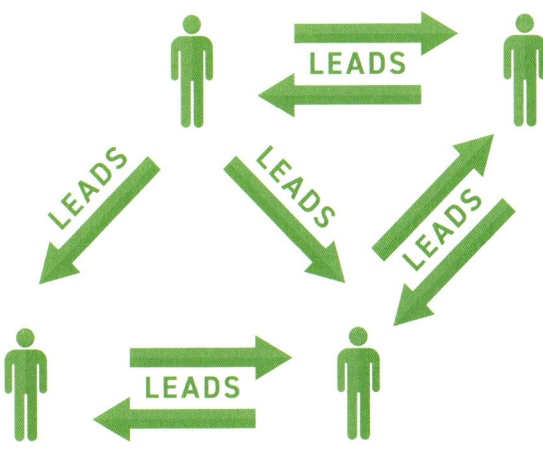

Fig 2. Illustration showing effective leadership works in all directions. Anyone can lead anyone.

A key aspect of sideways and upwards leadership is that you are leading people who are not obliged to obey. Where this is the case 'engaging others intellectually and emotionally' is particularly important because you can only lead these people if they choose to be led by you. Asymmetric leadership relies on people skills and personality rather than position.

Ideas and energy can be valid and powerful whatever the grade or rank of the initiator, and in many organisations there is little or no correlation between grade and intellect; often it is age rather than ability which accounts for a person's level in a hierarchy.

Part One **Leadership**

"The organisations that will survive and thrive will be those that foster acts of leadership throughout the system, rather than assuming leaders only exist at the top."

Max Weber [3]

I heard a great example of asymmetric leadership at work a few years ago when I was helping some delegates from clothing manufacturer, WL Gore. They told me that anyone in their company can start and lead a project if it is in line with the company's goals, as long as they can convince a panel who review proposals and can gather the necessary team to work on it.

> **Exercise**
>
> *See if you can create a flow diagram like the one in this section that shows how leadership flows in your work environment.*

- *Write your name at the centre of the page and add the names of up to eight people you interact closely with.*
- *Draw lines showing how leadership flows within this group.*
- *You might use thick lines and thin lines to help define the volume and weight of leadership applied.*

Me

If all the lines flow from senior staff downhill, then your organisation is hierarchical, and creativity will be stifled. If there is a healthy number of leadership lines stretching upwards, then there is a high level of creativity, and staff will feel connected to the organisation's purpose.

Part One **Leadership**

1.4 The Need for a Clear and Compelling Purpose

'Ad Unum Omnes' – all to one end

A team is only really a team if it has purpose. A group of travellers on a bus would not be a team, but if that bus were to be become stranded in a snowstorm, then survival would become a clear and compelling purpose and the group of travellers might feel motivated to work together as a team.

The importance of purpose was defined a long time ago. At the turn of the 19th Century, Carl Von Clausewitz identified 'selection and maintenance of the aim' as the first, and paramount principle of war[4]. History is threaded by clear and compelling purposes which have given focus to human activity.

Effective leaders and high-performing organisations are always clear what they are working towards.

Think of a sports team from an isolated community. If it had no competitions to enter, or no other teams to play against, they would have no reason to train or improve. Trying to win the cup, or beat the competition gives them their purpose – it gives them a reason to train hard and to develop their teamwork and tactics. Clear and compelling purpose is a great motivator, and an absence of meaningful purpose has the opposite effect.

The Leadership Book by Neil Jurd

Think of a company that makes regional newspapers. If you were to ask several people in the company what their purpose is, the likelihood is that they would all have a slightly different answer. This is because different people and departments within the newspaper office will have different perspectives. Some might say to produce a paper, others might argue that it is to sell advertising, and others might say that their purpose is to make an editorial point. All these separate visions of what the purpose is will work subtly against each other. This will lead to competition within the team for resources and attention. This will create friction between departments and will dilute the force and focus of the organisation.

To avoid internal friction and to drive activity, leaders need to work hard to define the purpose of their team or organisation. That purpose should be 'clear and compelling'. Simple enough that everyone in the team will understand it – not too long and written in plain language and emotionally engaging enough so that people will want to work for it.

A structure that works well is for the statement to have two elements to it: 'What and Why'. The 'What' guides activity, the 'Why' fuels emotional engagement.

Here are two of examples of what a Clear and Compelling Purpose could look like:

Examples

Large Youth Organisation
We are aiming to be the most exciting and inclusive youth organisation in the region (WHAT), in order to attract new members and so have a positive impact on as many young people as possible (WHY).

Newspaper
To provide the most trustworthy and up to date source of news in the region (WHAT), in order to be the media outlet of choice for readers and advertisers (WHY).

A well-defined purpose can be incredibly powerful. It can inspire and energise, but only if it is well understood within the organisation. Too often the purpose gets lost in corporate documents; even though people know it exists, the purpose is not a lived experience. This is where you, as a leader need to ensure that everyone not only understands the purpose, but that they are excited by it and focussed on it.

The purpose will need to be discussed regularly to keep it in the forefront of people's minds. It should be brought into meetings, linked to people's objectives, and referenced in plans. All work should be guided by the same clear and compelling purpose.

If you get the purpose right, it will energise the organisation, pull people together, focus resources and give meaning to people's work.

Exercise

Think about the organisation you lead or are part of. Try to define its Clear and Compelling Purpose?

The Clear and Compelling Purpose of my organisation is:

Part 1.
....
....
(WHAT)
....

Part 2.
....
....
(WHY)
....

The Leadership Book by Neil Jurd

"The effective leader considers themselves to just be another team member, but one whose function is leading."

NJ

Part One **Leadership**

1.5 Leading with Humility

"Humility is not thinking less of yourself. It is thinking of yourself less."
CS Lewis[5]

The Royal Military Academy Sandhurst is one of the world's oldest and most prestigious leadership training centres; I trained and later taught there. It has been developing leaders since 1801, with Winston Churchill being one of the best-known graduates. The academy motto is 'Serve to Lead'[6] and in this section I'm going to explain what that means, and why service is such an important aspect of positive leadership.

Fig 3. Sketch of The Royal Military Academy Sandhurst.

Although there might be some privileges to being a leader; enough to attract and keep the best people, a good leader does not seek these privileges that set them apart from the people they lead.

At the heart of this ethos is the idea is that leadership is a role in the team, and that the effective leader considers themselves to just be another team member, but one whose function is leading. So, leadership is an act of service: serving the people you work with and serving the purpose that your team is working towards.

In effective leadership the focus is outwards, on others and on the objective. If a leader's principal aim is to serve themselves, that is toxic and narcissistic leadership – using position for personal gain.

In the Serve to Lead style, leaders care for the people in their team. At Sandhurst, when I was a cadet, we were also taught to check our soldiers' feet for blisters and injury after long marches. There is very little glamour in checking smelly feet. But by caring for the team, the leader makes sure they are fit and able to focus on the objective. The team notice and people feel safer working for leaders that care.

In your environment, checking your team's feet might be unwelcome attention. But there will be other ways that you can show you care for your team. You can make sure they have the best possible working conditions. And that they get a decent amount of time away from the office – encouraging people to go home on time, and to take their annual leave. If you care for your people, they will be better able to focus on whatever purpose your team is working towards.

An important way in which this style of leader serves the team is by working to be highly competent at what they do. A leader is honoured by the fact that others are willing to follow them. If the team is going to give its best in its specialisations, the leader needs to be at their absolute best as a leader.

To be the best possible leader needs study and preparation (this book is a good start). A leader needs to know how to do their technical role whatever their trade is and needs to study leadership. Things that might help are watching TED talks, reading, going on courses, and having coaching.

Finally, a huge part of this style of leadership is using personality rather than position to get things done. It is about connecting with people, as equals, forming personal connections that create trust and mutual understanding. This style of leadership implies humility and is underwritten by decency and competence.

Leaders with humility lead from within rather than from above the team.

> **Exercise**
>
> *Take a few minutes to think about these points:*
> - *When has a leader cared for you, and what effect did that have?*
> - *What changes could you make to serve your team more effectively?*

1.6 False Leadership

I am sometimes asked to account for the success of influential people whose leadership style is so different from the inclusive and positive leadership style that I advocate. The usual examples are self-serving politicians whose style is divisive and egotistical, or further along the same scale, dictators, and despots. But of course, there are self-centred, narcissistic, and egotistic people thriving in senior positions in all walks of life. You may know some and their energy and impact are likely to be negative.

These people inhabit senior positions, but their intrinsic motivation is usually self-centred; they lead in order to serve their own purposes. For their own recognition and wealth, rather than for any greater good. In my experience, these people do not lead in the truest sense of the word. I call this 'false leadership'; it is presented as leadership, and it looks like leadership from a distance, but it lacks the meaning, substance and positivity of the real thing.

When you look closely, you will find that rather than positively engaging with others, the false-leader's style is to dominate or manipulate, often in pursuit of unclear, immoral or negative objectives. There will often be a significant disparity between the false-leader's real objectives, and the version presented to followers.

True leadership has authentic foundations, is honest, inclusive and focussed on positive impact. Where a person in a position of authority doesn't meet these conditions, then it is likely they are misusing their position to dominate and manipulate.

1.7 Universal Leadership Behaviours

In leadership development, there is often a focus on the qualities that a leader should possess. The lists that emerge can be extensive and overwhelming. The United States Marine Corps defines 14 leadership traits, while the Centre for Creative Leadership defines 10 characteristics and qualitie[8]. Lists like this can give the impression that to be a leader, you must be an exceptional being.

But that just isn't so: most people have it in them to lead. If you have an idea and you engage others to help you to turn that idea into reality, you are leading. So, the act of leading often is not dramatic or newsworthy; it could be as simple as arranging a rota to look after a vulnerable neighbour, or a leaving present for a valued colleague. Of course, your leadership could also be more significant: leading a department, a school, a charity, or company.

There are just four core leadership behaviours which are universally found in people at all levels who have a positive leadership effect. These are behaviours that all of us could have; it is up to us to choose whether to adopt and apply them.

First, they always behave honestly

Leaders create teams, be they formal structures or informal alliances. And trust is an essential part of high-performing cultures. People will be drawn to support and work with a leader whose word can always be trusted, and who behaves with integrity. Conversely, any dishonest behaviour undermines the spirit of trust around that leader. Political manoeuvring, office affairs, fiddling expenses or any other form of dishonesty undermines a leader's trust and credibility. An element of being honest is to behave with authenticity; by authenticity I mean just being yourself rather than playing the part you think your role requires.

Second, leaders sometimes behave bravely

Not like a firefighter entering a burning building, although at the extreme end of the scale it could mean that. But more likely at a much more mundane but still scary level. From time to time something difficult must be done; a tough decision has to be made, or a problem confronted. This is about social rather than physical risk, but it is something people often shy away from. In my experience, leaders are more likely to show moral courage when they are passionate about the clear and compelling purpose they are working towards.

Third, leaders are often selfless

By this I mean that they will often, put the interests of others ahead of their own interests. This might mean helping one of your team get an upgraded company car, or it could mean staying late to help somebody else with their work. I say 'often' selfless and not 'always', because at times a leader needs to care for themselves.

Fourth, leaders often take the time to think

Leaders have a lot to think about; the greater the clear and compelling purpose they are leading, the more there is to think about. The things they will think about might include the overall purpose they are trying to achieve, the people in their team and the budget. Creating and using time to think is really important. If the leader does not make thinking a regular behaviour, it is unlikely any other member of the team will do so, and the organisation or team is literally mindless.

In my experience, if a leader can apply these behaviours; to be honest always, to think and to be selfless often, and to sometimes be brave, then they will be setting an example that inspires others and at the same time makes others feel safe.

The Danger of Being Selfless

The British Army lists 'Selfless Commitment' amongst its values and standards. I very deliberately wrote that leaders are 'often' selfless, having seen several of my friends in senior military appointments become overwhelmed by their workload and responsibilities, cornered by the need to show selfless commitment. In any meaningful endeavour there are times when selfless commitment is necessary, usually at pivotal moments and for short periods. In military terms this is when deployed on operations. In business it could be in the days leading up to a product launch. In a school it could be the first few weeks of the new school year. But selfless commitment is not sustainable. Leaders also need to create space for their own welfare: health, fitness, family, and relationships. It is these times of nurture that prepare us for short periods of intense and demanding focus.

The Leadership Book by Neil Jurd

"We all need space; unless we have it, we cannot reach that sense of quiet in which whispers of better things come to us gently"

Octavia Hill [9]

1.8 Leadership Behaviour – The Need to Clear Space

Thinking Time - Leaders need to think

One of the most important functions of a leader is to think. The direction, structure and culture of the organisation are all the leader's responsibility, so there is a lot to think about.

Often thinking is a lot harder than it should be and is even sometimes frowned upon. People often mistake taking time to think as being ineffective. Organisational culture tends to carry people along, and the day becomes quickly filled with meetings and video calls. Often these meetings will run back to back with little or no recovery space.

One client of mine captures it nicely when he talks about 'being busy fools'. People are too busy to use their brains. Their high activity-rate makes them less intelligent and less productive; work is approached mindlessly as people confuse being present with being effective. Senior staff often find themselves present in meetings of limited relevance, where they have no impact, conforming to expectations instead of using their time well. How often do you find yourself in meetings wondering why you were invited?

And then there is technology and the many interruptions that it allows: emails, texts, and the incessant chatter of social media. Endless messages preventing the brain from entering deep thought. We check our phone every few minutes (if you have never given this any thought, I challenge you to notice how many times you check yours in the next hour), and our social media apps aim to make us spend more time in an enduring state of distraction. We have access to too much information. This is sometimes called cognitive overload, and it overpowers our ability to think clearly.

So, in the work environment, most people are distracted by two things: mindless organisational culture, and addictive technology. It is often impossible to get any meaningful thinking done.

And if you cannot think, your leadership effect is severely limited. You can serve as a manager without much thought, but not as an effective leader.

This distracting and mindless working culture can be hard to resist, but if you want to lead you have to break out of it and find the time and space to engage your brain. In the army whilst I was serving in Iraq during 2006 and 2007, I worked for Lieutenant Colonel David Golding, a remarkably clear-thinking boss who used to make time most days to practice guitar. He told me that he did this to help clear his head and help him create space for ideas.

The best ideas often come to our minds when they are clear. You might have already experienced this: a great eureka moment when you have been walking the dog, riding your bike, or even lying in bed. Thomas Edison used to operate in the space on the very edge of sleep. He would sit in an armchair, with a brass ball in each hand. As he would start to fall asleep, the balls would drop, which would then wake him up. He found that he was most creative in this state of almost total relaxation.

How you can create space will depend on your circumstances. If you are working from home, it might mean taking time away from the computer and video conferences. At work you might close your office door, or find a meeting room, or you might need to physically leave the office, turn your computer off, or go somewhere and not carry your phone with you. Whatever it is that you need to do, try hard to create the conditions where you can think. And repeat the process often.

At first a form of cultural friction might hold you back, and you may need to show some moral courage to resist that. It is for the greater good that you challenge mindlessness, create time and space, use your brain, and encourage others to do likewise.

> **Exercise**
> *You might like to consider how much time you currently allow yourself to think, and how much of your time is spent in unproductive activity. And then try to list 3 changes you can make that will help redress the balance.*
>
> 1. ....
> 2. ....
> 3. ....

1.9 Different Leadership Styles

Think about some of the leaders you have worked with over the years, about what they did well and what they did less well. I have had the privilege of working for some superb leaders, and the horror of a few who were less impressive. In my coaching work I would say that at least half of the problems that I have helped people to resolve relate to difficult bosses.

Some leaders just get it right: their impact is well-directed, their presence inspires confidence, they know where they are going, and they empower and trust their team. I'll say more about positive leaders towards the end of this section.

There are other leaders who are in the wrong place, doing the wrong work, creating friction and distraction. Their involvement causes delay and confusion and, in their absence, people feel hesitant and confused.

In this section I have described a few different leadership stereotypes; whilst the first four are negative, the last is an example of what 'good' looks like. As you read these profiles, you might recognise elements of your own style. Spotting them in the first four profiles is useful: you have identified changes you can make to develop your leadership. Most people have elements of a number of these profiles.

5 Leadership Profiles

The first type of leader I refer to as **The Comfort Worker**. This leader throws themselves into detail and tasks – working hard, but at the wrong stuff. Often doing the sort of work they did when they were more junior: work they are good at but which has little leadership effect. The cover story for this avoidant leader is that they are 'leading by example' yet they have little leadership effect. An example might be the IT director fixing faults on their own computer. This style of working is often the result of the person genuinely not understanding their role as a leader, feeling slightly guilty and attempting to prove their worth in other ways. The Comfort Worker has little impact beyond the small task they are focussed on, but as a leader's key role is to engage in work that delivers leadership effect, they must leave their Comfort Work behind to become more impactful.

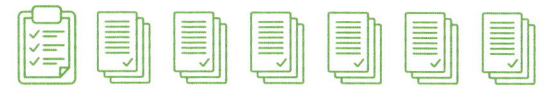

The second profile is **The Attender**. This leader mindlessly follows a programme and routine of meetings, totally stuck within a busy process. The day, week and year are planned out – financial planning committee, inclusion committee, strategic planning group and so on. Their calendar is full. There are crumbs in the keyboard and this person is an early starter and late finisher. This leader will usually seem harassed and is very much part of the corporate furniture, but nobody is quite sure what they do. They have a high profile but somehow lack impact. The Attender needs to take control of their working life and define what is important, prioritising work that contributes to the clear and compelling purpose.

The third profile is **The Meddler**. This leader spends their day micro-managing others – closely directing, monitoring, and checking the work of others. Often this leader does not understand the difference between leading and managing and they justify their position as a leader by exerting their authority over the detail. This type of leadership behaviour is very damaging. It undermines trust and creativity whilst disempowering and demoralising the team. While a leader is getting involved in somebody else's job, they are not actually doing their own. The cover story here may be that they are supporting the team, but the reality is that they are smothering it, discouraging initiative and innovation. The Meddler needs to become comfortable trusting others and must learn to focus on the bigger picture of purpose and strategy.

The fourth profile I call **The Deserter**. You may have seen this character, but more than likely not: they are simply not there when you need them. This sort of leader goes absent without leave or is too busy to see you. They might always be at conferences, or on a train, or working from home – none of these things are bad of course, but with the deserter it is just one thing after another. They are working on their own, often on quite irrelevant initiatives, instead of being where they are needed to support, guide, and decide. They are difficult to tie down for a decision and impossible to engage in serious, difficult, or challenging decisions. The cover story for this type of avoidant leader is that they are 'empowering others'. This sort of leader needs to be more engaged, give more clarity and structure to their team and be willing and available to make decisions.

Those were four examples of negative leadership profiles; let me now bring together some of the qualities and behaviours I would associate with an effective leader.

The Effective Leader focuses their time on activities that have a clear leadership impact and will spend quite a lot of time thinking. They may go for a walk, take a few hours off, or take their team away to reflect and plan. But they create time and space to use their brain. They are brave and do what needs to be done and do not worry too much how it looks to an imagined audience. They have their effect with and through others, so devote enough time to connecting with people to keep them engaged on working towards the clear and compelling purpose.

This leader builds trust, and develops a culture where people support each other. Time is spent mentoring, coaching, and developing others. People are made to feel useful and trusted and never diminished. This leader is calm and effective, bringing out the best in others.

Within this leader's team, people have considerable freedom within boundaries, but the leader checks in with them to offer support and to keep connection. This leader is comfortable being themselves – leading through personal connection, with minimal use of positional power.

This leader embodies the principles and ideas in this book by engaging others emotionally and intellectually in the pursuit of a clear and compelling purpose.

Exercise
Which of these leadership styles most closely matches your own? Can you list 3 things you could change about your leadership style to make it more effective?

1.
2.
3.

Part One **Leadership**

"Always be tactful and well-mannered and teach your subordinates to do the same. Avoid excessive sharpness or harshness of voice, which usually indicates the man who has shortcomings of his own."

Field Marshall Rommel[10]

1.10 Keeping Leadership Positive – Leading in the Blue Zone

The way a leader behaves will have an enormous impact on the morale and performance of the people they lead. The mood and attitude of one person influences those with whom they come into contact with. A smile is usually returned with a smile, and tension is equally infectious. This effect is particularly strong when the person smiling or creating tension is in a leadership position. So, because leaders deliver much of their effect by engaging with others, the quality and tone of that engagement matters a great deal.

The attitude and mood of the leader has a major impact on the culture and performance of the team or the organisation. The leader can trigger positivity or negativity. As scientist Isaac Newton identified, every action has an equal and opposite reaction[11]. As leaders, we reap what we sow and get back what we put in. A leader who brings positive leadership and behaviour into the team will get positive energy and behaviour back from them.

In this model which I have designed to explain this concept there are two zones: Blue and Red. Positive actions sit in the Blue Zone, and negative actions sit in the Red Zone. The positive things a leader can do, which are in the 'Blue Zone' which will bring out the best in others. Conversely, the negative actions of a leader in the 'Red Zone' will bring out the worst in their team. The behaviour of other people becomes a feedback loop to the leader, which can be either positive or negative.

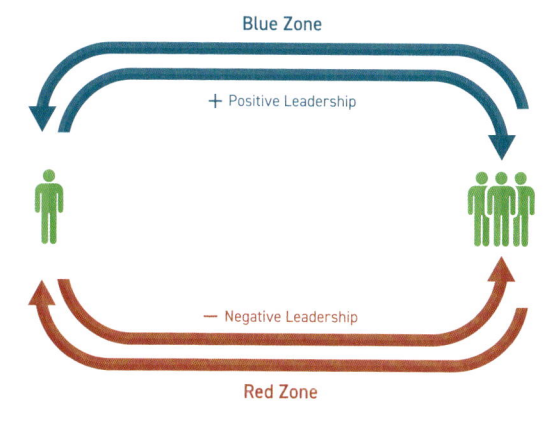

Fig 4. Model showing how positive and negative behaviour can have a positive and negative effect on a team (Source: Neil Jurd).

Red Zone Leadership

Red Zone leadership takes many forms but is characterised by any form of leadership behaviour that has a detrimental effect on the people within the team. Arrogance, rudeness or dismissiveness of others diminishes people and reduces their self-worth and willingness to engage. It undermines trust and mutual understanding in the team and makes people more status conscious.

A leader with a tendency to attach blame to mistakes will stifle initiative. People will avoid responsibility and will refer trivial decisions to their boss rather than risk being blamed for potential failure. The result is that nothing happens without the leader's involvement. The blame culture might also make team members turn on each other to find other scapegoats for perceived failure. The end result is that internal friction interferes with performance.

Other leaders might confuse activity with effect, which creates a bustling atmosphere where very little actually gets done. The busyness might overwhelm the leader and the team. There will be lots of committees and meetings and supporting paperwork. This could be quite a stressful environment, but it will not be an effective one.

There are many ways in which a leader can behave negatively, some trivial, some significant. But any negative behaviour will have a negative impact on team performance.

> **Example**
> *I once worked for a major who used to shout at me and other junior officers to make his point. He once shouted because a tin of paint had gone missing, another time because of a problem with a radio battery. Often, we junior officers had no real idea what we had done wrong; I remember on one occasion standing to attention under a barrage of words, hoping I would grasp why he was angry before he became even more annoyed. He in turn worked for a Lieutenant Colonel known for being arrogant and personally ambitious. Everything changed with the arrival of a new commander: a talented and emotionally aware leader whose presence and style transformed the culture of the Battalion. My immediate boss relaxed, and the same effect was felt across the organisation.*

Blue Zone Leadership

Positive behaviour will lead to positive results. So, at the basic level, being kind, decent, patient and caring will help develop strong and supportive relationships.

If the leader gives people freedom and resists the temptation to meddle, then a feeling of engagement, trust and empowerment is likely to develop. The team will work in a way that requires little management. They will think, create ideas and make decisions. All of this helps the leader become more effective as they are free to lead, rather than managing the detail.

Other positive behaviour would include communicating openly and honestly, involving people in thinking and developing ideas and just behaving decently and kindly: no doubt you can think of many more, all of which help build a positive atmosphere. The way the leader behaves has a very direct impact on the culture and performance of the team that they lead.

> **Example**
> *I have seen several superb examples of Blue Zone Leadership from my good friend Nigel Williams. Nigel is a calm, humorous and gentle man and is one of Scotland's most experienced mountain leaders. He and I have spent weeks together on skis in Norway. Early one year we were with three inexperienced skiers in a mountainous area. Injury had slowed us down and we were still out after night had fallen. Temperatures were below zero and dropping fast. We could not find the hut where we were to spend the night and there was no other accommodation for 20 miles. The mood in the group became uncomfortable; tired and inexperienced skiers were frustrated and scared at the idea of a night outdoors in the Norwegian wilds. The hut was close but hidden in woods the other side of a deep snow-filled river valley crossed by a single-track bridge. Without knowing our exact position there was a strong chance we would miss the hut, and the situation, which required precise navigation would become serious and dangerous. In this pressured and demanding situation, Nigel remained perfectly calm, looking after and reassuring the group. Nigel's attitude and calm positivity, combined with his brilliance as a navigator and experience on dangerous ground, is a classic example of Blue Zone leadership, creating a sense of safety in what was without doubt a dangerous situation.*

Positive leadership behaviours bring out the best in the team. They reassure, empower, and energise. Negative leadership behaviours stifle and supress, making the team less effective. Understanding the positive or negative effect your leadership can have on a team will enable you to be the best version of yourself.

Reflection

What can you do to maximise the positive behaviour in your leadership practice?

Part Two People

PART TWO

PEOPLE

THIS SECTION WILL HELP YOU TO UNDERSTAND
AND GET THE BEST OUT OF YOURSELF,
AND OTHERS

2.1 Self-Knowledge and Self-Control

"One conquers who conquers oneself" Publilius Syrus [13]

As a leader, it is important to have self-knowledge and self-control before you can effectively lead others. This section explains that concept and introduces my interpretation of the Merrill and Reid [12] Social Styles model which will give a framework for understanding yourself and others.

You have may have seen or even worked for leaders who lack self-knowledge and self-control. I have worked for a few, and never enjoyed the experience. They will often be incredibly thick-skinned and blissfully unaware of the effect that their behaviour has on others.

Effective leaders know themselves well, and work hard to apply their strengths and to address or compensate for their weaknesses. They use this knowledge to grow and develop their skills, and they might choose to create a team around them whose strengths and talents compensate for their own weaknesses. A leader with self-knowledge and self-control will understand their own emotions and feelings, will pay attention to them, and will be able to discuss them with others.

> **Case study**
>
> *Ishy is the Headteacher of a thriving sixth-form college. He is a kind and thoughtful man, popular amongst the staff. However, under pressure he used to became irritable, with a tendency to blame others for mistakes. After focusing on understanding and changing this behaviour he has learned to control the fear of failure that drove his negative response to pressure. Now before responding under pressure, Ishy calms himself by creating the time and space to think. Sometimes this just means slowing his breathing and taking a step back, or it can mean hours or days of reflection. The culture in the senior leadership team of the college is now much more positive, and Ishy feels much happier now he has better control of his behaviour under pressure.*

The Leadership Book by Neil Jurd

"If you know yourself well, you will understand what drives you. You will be able to harness the strengths that brings, and be able to control the potential down-side of your personality."

NJ

A leader who does not know themselves, or who lacks self-control will generate a form of turbulence that makes others feel unsafe. Their behaviour will be unpredictable and uncontrolled emotions will sometimes lead to outbursts that damage relationships and leave people hurt. Often these behaviours are driven by fear, or other undefined negative emotions. Leaders who lack self-control, often blame or find it hard to trust others and might tend towards micro-management.

If you know yourself well, you will understand what drives you. You will be able to harness the strengths that brings, and be able to control the potential down-side of your personality. So, for example, if you know that you prefer to be task focussed then you might choose to work harder to consider the interests and feelings if people in your decision making.

Whatever you are like, understanding yourself and making use of that knowledge will make you a more effective leader. Being able to understand others in the same way will help you to connect with them and get the best from them. There is a simple model in the next section that will give you a framework for understanding yourself and others. In chapter 2.3 of this book I outline other tools you can use to further develop and use this understanding.

2.2 The Merril and Reid Social Styles Model

At the beginning of the book I mentioned Field Marshall Lord Slim's statement that 'Leadership is just plain you'. In this chapter I am going to explain a simple model which will help you to understand exactly who 'plain you' is.

The model is Merrill and Reid's Social Styles Model. This model will help you to understand yourself; just as importantly, in so doing, you will learn to apply this knowledge to those in your immediate team.

It is important to understand that there is no 'right place' to be on this model. Any position on the model comes with costs and benefits. Most of us are able to 'stretch' between different positions on the model, but we will have a preference for where we feel most comfortable; we will also have a place on the model where we go under pressure.

The horizontal axis defines whether you tend to be focussed on task or people. If you prefer to engage with the task, you are above the line; if you prefer to engage with people then you are below the line.

The Leadership Book by Neil Jurd

Analyst
- Steady pace, slower to act
- Organises people and activities
- Less concerned about relationships
- Acts with caution
- Objective, structured approach

Driver
- Fast pace
- Seeks control
- Accepts risk in task and relationships
- Directive approach
- Frustrated by inaction

TASK

CONSULTS ← → DIRECTS

PEOPLE

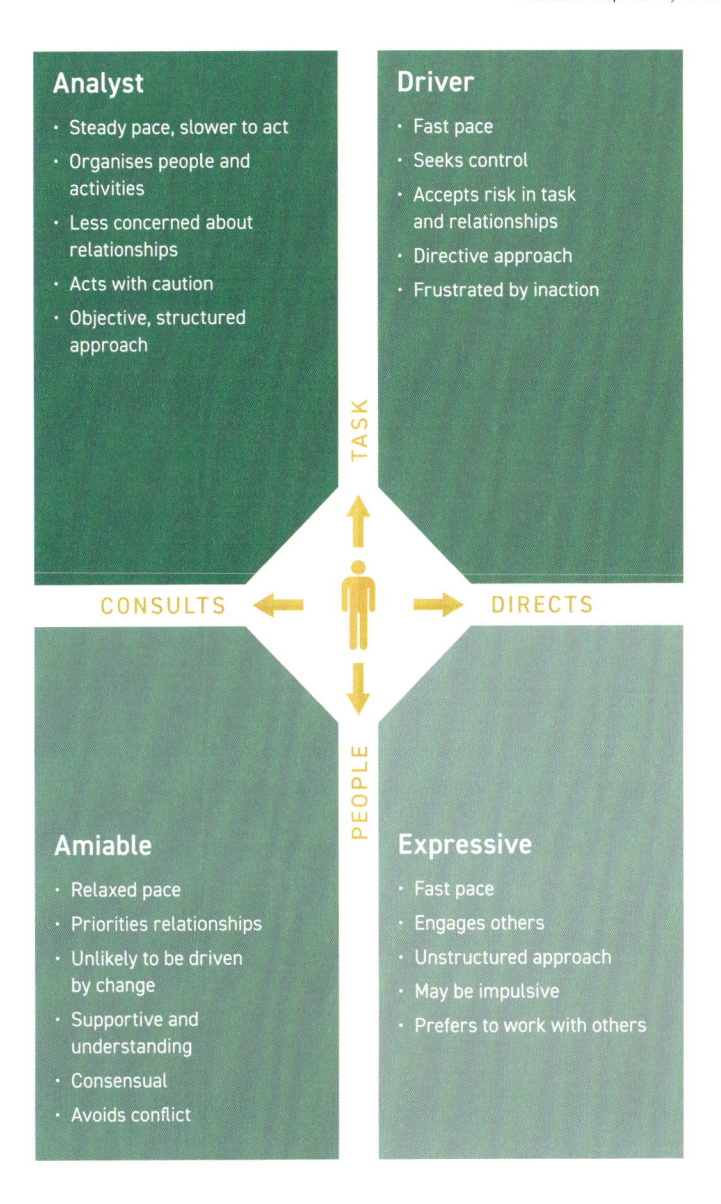

Amiable
- Relaxed pace
- Priorities relationships
- Unlikely to be driven by change
- Supportive and understanding
- Consensual
- Avoids conflict

Expressive
- Fast pace
- Engages others
- Unstructured approach
- May be impulsive
- Prefers to work with others

Fig.5 The Merrill and Reid's Social Styles Model.

The vertical axis divides whether you prefer to direct or consult. If you prefer to gather consensus and information, you are to the left, where you consult. If you prefer pushing the activity and people, you are to the right and you direct.

The model breaks down into four quadrants.

In the top right there is the task focused director, or the **'Driver'**. These are people who work at a fast pace, who seek to control the activity, and are willing to take risks with people and tasks. They will tend to direct people and become frustrated by inaction.

In the bottom right of the model is the people focussed director, or the **'Expressive'**. Expressives will also work at a fast pace, but will engage more with others, and will have a less structured approach. They might be described as impulsive. Overall, these people will enjoy working with other people.

The bottom left of the model is the people focussed consultor, or the **'Amiable'**. These people will be happier working at a more relaxed, slower pace, and will focus on keeping the relationships with people within their team positive. They are less likely to push change and more likely to fill a supportive and understanding role. They work in a consensual way and will prefer to avoid conflict where possible.

Finally, the top left of the model is dedicated to the task focussed consultor, or the **'Analyst'**. The analysts will also work at a slower pace, but because they like to get both the detail and the structure right. They plan well and tend to be highly organised, but are less concerned about the relationships that they form with their team. At times, they might appear to be cautious - even a bit bureaucratic-but will take a structured and logical approach to things.

The Leadership Book by Neil Jurd

How you can use the model

Start by thinking about where you would place yourself. Think about where you feel most comfortable, and which areas you can stretch to. Also consider the areas that make you feel uncomfortable.

When you are happy with where you sit as a leader on the model, use the information given to shape and adjust your behaviour accordingly. So, if you were heavily placed in one box, take a look in the others, and see if there is anything that you could try from these boxes which would make you a more effective leader. At the same time, consider the box you are in, and decide whether there are any aspects of your style that others might find difficult or frustrating.

The important thing to note is that it does not matter where you are on the model, simply that you use it to better understand yourself in order to develop your leadership.

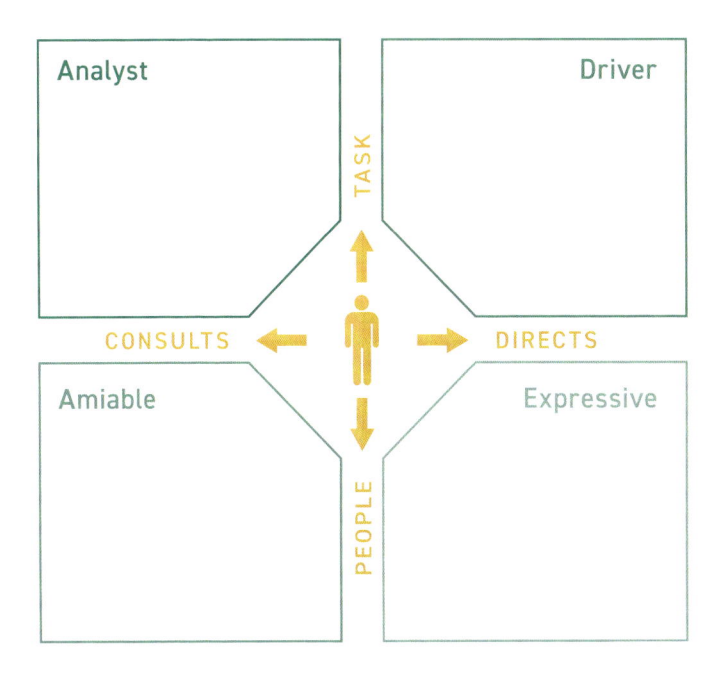

Analyst	Driver
Amiable	Expressive

TASK ↑
CONSULTS ← → DIRECTS
PEOPLE ↓

Part Two **People**

"Knowing yourself is the beginning of all wisdom"

Aristotle [14]

2.3 Some Ways to Get to Know Yourself

The Social Styles model in the previous section is a useful framework for understanding yourself and others. To get a better understanding of how you see yourself and how others see you, there are other tools you can use which will help you explore this area further. In this section I'm going to show how psychometric assessment, 360-degree profiling and coaching can help you and others to gain self-knowledge and to develop as leaders.

First, **Psychometric Assessments**. I have had a great deal of success using these in my professional practice. These tools are psychology based and help you to understand how you see yourself, compared to how a wide cross-section of other people see themselves. For instance, these tests will show whether you are more or less likely than others to prefer working in a team, or whether you prefer logical or emotional thought.

There are a wide range of free assessments available online or if you have a budget, the commercially available versions of the assessments are usually more accurate but take longer to complete.[15] Another well-regarded test is the 16 Personality Factors Assessment, known as 16PF.[16] To develop a good understanding of yourself, it is worth trying several different assessments and taking time to understand the results that are generated.

> **Example**
> *Recently I was working with an experienced undercover police officer whose working life is often dangerous and stressful. He has had a hard professional career and has often struggled to face up to challenging aspects of his own personality. Psychometric profiling created a huge breakthrough for him, which has enabled him to understand and control himself better and to build better relationships with his peers.*

A second method that you can use to learn more about yourself or, more specifically, how others see you, is to carry out a **360-degree assessment**. This means asking people around you to give feedback on how they see you. There are various formats for this, some structured, some less so.

You will find several free 360 feedback tools online, or you could keep it simple and just ask a few people whose opinion you value a few simple questions to help your development. These could be as simple as asking 'what do I do well? And 'what could I do better?'

Finally, you could gain self-knowledge by **working with a coach**. One of the primary roles of a coach is to help you understand yourself, by reflecting and sharing with you what they hear, see and perceive from your words and body language. A coach will bring your attention to your own unconscious beliefs and thought patterns, helping you to challenge and change unhelpful behaviour.

Coaching can be even more effective when it is supported by either of the tools I have already mentioned: 360 feedback and psychometric assessment. Many leadership development organisations now consider coaching, 360 feedback and psychometric profiling to be essential aspects of leadership development.

My final point on this subject is that – understanding yourself is not especially useful on its own. Whatever you learn about yourself only becomes useful when the knowledge is applied. If you discover that you tend to be very dominant, or very introverted or very extroverted, or very self-critical, you must work out how to apply that knowledge to become a more effective leader. Being mindful and working at our own personal development is an important part of developing as a leader.

Exercise

See if you can find two or three online psychometric assessments. Complete these and see what consistent themes appear in the reports they produce.

If you have a budget for development, consider investing in professional coaching, psychometric assessment and 360-degree feedback tools.

2.4 Understanding Different Perspectives

One of the key steps to becoming an effective leader is the ability to understand people. You will achieve the greatest impact as a leader through others, but to do this, you need to be able to connect with them. This part of the book will help you with that.

When you are trying to connect with people emotionally and intellectually (which is what effective leaders do) it is important to understand that each person is quite different from the next. It is easy to assume that our own views and opinions are so sensible and obvious that everyone must share them.

People usually see identical situations quite differently from each other, even people who know each other and get on well. These different viewpoints will often cause friction and misunderstanding between people. You sometimes hear statements like: 'it's obvious, why can't she see that?' or, 'surely he knew that would make me angry?' We assume that others see the world pretty much as we do. But that isn't usually the case; a decision that makes perfect sense to me might make no sense to you.

Often, when I run experiential learning sessions in which a team work together to try to solve a task. I stop them and ask all of the team members what emotion they are feeling at that moment. The result is usually a very wide range of emotions from strongly positive through to very negative, which usually comes as a shock to the leader.

HAPPY	FRUSTRATED	EXCITED
ENGAGED	EXHAUSTED	ENERGISED

Different viewpoints and misunderstanding can lead to a range of unexpressed emotions and feelings which sit below the surface of relationships and undermine cohesion: frustration, excitement, loneliness, disengagement, anger, and confusion are common ones.

To lead others effectively, emotional connection is important, so understanding and working to understand their viewpoints and feelings is an important part of winning their emotional engagement to make them feel safe and valued in the team. Some leaders I have worked with actually prefer not to know what others are thinking because 'if we know, then we have to do something about it'. To me, that seems a bit like the pilot of an airliner not wanting to find out why the engine is making a funny noise.

Often the outliers who are not engaged, or whose emotions don't align with what the leader expects or hopes to see in the team, feel the way they feel because they have spotted something or have a better idea. Understanding what others are thinking and exploring it can be a really effective way of developing a better plan or stopping yourself from leading the team in the wrong direction.

To help you understand the concept of why people differ, you might find the smartphones analogy useful.

2.5 The Smartphone Analogy

I suspect my use of the term 'smartphones' dates me, but in leadership and team development, there is some wisdom that comes with age (as well as some forgetfulness). My daughters found it very funny recently when I used the light on my phone to look at my watch. It took me several seconds to understand why they were laughing at me. But my life experiences are quite different from theirs and to me, at that time, my actions made perfect sense.

Imagine three brand-new identical phones: the latest and cleverest model, with more camera lenses, bought on the same day, by three friends. I suggest this analogy because my daughter and her two best friends all have the same make and model of phone but can instantly tell them apart. The phones are as different as the owners.

Initially those phones are identical, but over time the differences between them would increase. They would have different apps installed, hold different photos, and have different connections in the address book. They would have different covers or protective cases, different chips and dents and different screen savers. The phones might even have different navigational programmes which might offer quite different routes to the same destination.

People are like that, even though we are the same species and almost identical – genetics and life experiences have programmed each of us slightly differently. We are interested in different things and we develop our individual core beliefs and values. We suffer different chips and dents. We present ourselves differently, we see the world differently and we navigate situations differently. When I drive, I prefer the scenic route and avoid traffic; I have friends who would always choose the most direct route and would endure traffic.

Similar people see things differently. This is inevitable, but not always apparent. These differences in perspective can be extremely useful if they are understood and considered; they lead to creativity and new ideas. However, when these differences are not understood or explored, they can lead to friction, misunderstanding and misalignment. Effective leaders understand that people will have unique viewpoints, and they are willing to explore and understand those viewpoints.

2.6 Finding Out What Others are Thinking

You might be wondering how do you get to understand what others are thinking or feeling? Well you don't usually need to be a mind-reader or an FBI interrogator.

There are two aspects to this: Over Time, and In the Moment:

First, I'll talk about understanding people over time: this is about building meaningful connections between team members. This means setting the conditions for honesty, creating trust in the team and building a positive atmosphere. This might include spending time with people and talking with them, so you understand them, and so they understand you. It also means trying to understand their background, their beliefs – what excites them and what makes them angry.

Second, understanding people in the moment: here the best way to understand what people are feeling is, kindly and unthreateningly, to ask them. It really is that easy. Create the conditions and craft a kind challenge designed to connect with their thinking. You might say something like 'let's just stop for a few minutes, maybe get a cup of tea – and then let's talk about how we feel about this plan'. And then as their perspective emerges, you need to understand and consider their point, and take it into account. Often for people, having their perspective understood and considered is enough.

If you do this, you'll help make sure that the whole team feels engaged, included and positive about what you are working on and you won't be pushing people against their will or missing out on important information and ideas.

"Engaging with others is a core leadership activity. The aim is to really get to know people: to break down the hierarchy, bureaucracy and status consciousness around you in order to form really meaningful connections."

NJ

2.7 Connecting with People

"The greatest leader is not necessarily the one who does the greatest things. He is the one that gets the people to do the greatest things"

Ronald Reagan[17]

Effective leaders need to be good at connecting with people. Even if your nature is introverted and you lean more towards engaging in a task than connecting with people, as a leader, connecting with people is essential. Why is it so important? Think back to the definition of leadership that underpins this course: leaders achieve things far beyond what they could do alone, by engaging others intellectually and emotionally in pursuit of a clear and compelling purpose.

Engaging others is a core leadership activity, an effective use of your time, which can also be interesting and enjoyable. By engaging with people, I mean really connect. The aim is to get to know people: to break down the hierarchy, bureaucracy and status consciousness around you in order to form really meaningful connections. Connect with the people in your team and the people who interact with your team.

In chapter 2.9 I explain the communication pyramid, which explains the different levels at which we communicate. At the base of the pyramid is the lowest and least engaging level; 'Ritual and Cliché. As communications improve, the model then climbs through 'Facts and Information', 'Ideas and Judgements' then 'Emotions and Feelings' through to 'Peak'.

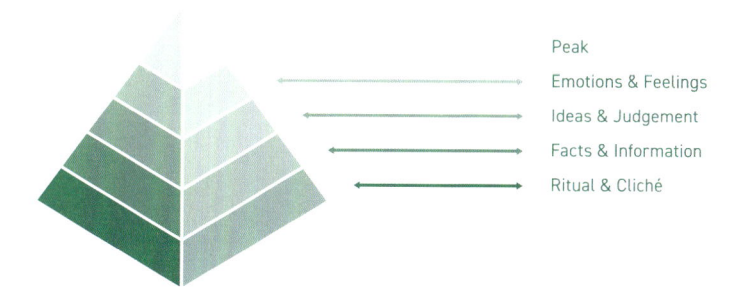

Peak
Emotions & Feelings
Ideas & Judgement
Facts & Information
Ritual & Cliché

Fig 6. Levels of Communication Pyramid, Father John Powell.

The higher up the communications model we climb, the better our connection with people – so an effective use of a leader's time is to talk with people and climb the pyramid with them. However busy you are as a leader, it is important to prioritise connecting with people. This will be an alien concept in many organisations, where harvesting emails and filling space at meetings takes precedence over engaging with people. Becoming an effective leader involves challenging unhelpful organisational culture, so this could be a good place to start.

Let me start with a quick guide to connecting with people, to which you can add your own ideas.

First, an essential skill for a leader is remembering names. Knowing someone's name creates a broadband connection to them and when you really try, it is surprisingly easy. Napoleon knew the names of many of his soldiers and in return he was immensely popular with them and they showed him great loyalty.

Running experiential leadership development courses, I taught myself to learn the names of all 30 delegates on a course in the first hour. I have an average memory so this took some effort, but I realised that getting names right was the most important thing I could do to help build a good relationship with the people on the course.

A good way to build connections is to visit your team where they work and spend some time with them. This way you are meeting on their territory, where they feel most comfortable. This takes a lot of the friction and interference out of the process and allows a more relaxed and honest level of connection. Walking around is always good as you meet people and see things that are not obvious from your desk.

If you work in a dispersed team, the same principle applies: meet with people often and in a way that removes status from the engagement. Connecting through video conferencing or on the phone is a little bit harder, so to compensate for that, you must try a little bit harder. Be a little more animated and work hard to invite people's opinions and to encourage them to speak.

I have a few 'rules' which apply to connecting which might help you.

The 5 Rules of Connecting

1. Always accept a cup of tea or coffee when offered. This lets people know that you have time for them.

2. Be yourself. Do not be tempted to hide behind your position or status. Instead, be relaxed, smile and look people in the eye.

3. Be present, and occasionally take notes. Take the time to ask questions about them, and how they are feeling. And switch off or silence digital devices for the duration of the meeting.

4. Listen much more than you talk. Try not to take any criticism personally and become defensive of company policy or your own decisions. Just listen to what people are saying and try to understand what is important to them.

5. If there is time, talk simply and consistently about what you are trying to achieve in the organisation.

Effective leaders work hard to build and nurture great relationships. If you are a shy or introverted person this can feel uncomfortable, but the benefit is worth the cost. You will make people feel connected, engaged, valued and safe.

There are things you can do right away to start building great connections. The main thing is to create time to get to know people, listen to their ideas and opinions, and be open to their perspectives.

> **Exercise**
>
> *Can you list 5 things you could do in the coming month to build stronger connections with your team?*
>
> 1.
> 2.
> 3.
> 4.
> 5.

2.8 Relationships, Trust and Mutual Understanding

Relationships, Trust and Mutual Understanding are essential elements of a positive working culture, and a positive culture is essential in a high-performing team. You'll find more about culture in high performing teams in the model of Team Development at chapter 3.6.

Napoleon said that morale is three times more important than physical strength; and more recently the phrase 'culture eats strategy for breakfast' has been used within Ford Motor Group to emphasise the importance of getting the atmosphere right.

In a high-performing organisation you would expect to find a high level of trust and mutual understanding based on strong and positive relationships. If the team is hierarchical, then this exists between layers. And if there are different departments, then strong relationships, trust and mutual understanding link them.

Friction Between Layers

However, high-performing teams like this are rare. In most organisations there is friction and misunderstanding, with divisions forming between layers of management, and between departments in an organisation.

What might this look like? Typically, senior leaders might become detached from reality - not understanding the problems that exist on the shopfloor. Junior staff will feel unappreciated, disconnected and misunderstood. The middle managers will feel under pressure from all directions, unable to please the senior bosses or the junior staff. Between departments, there will be tension and internal competition, often described as working in silos. Energy that should be directed towards organisational success is wasted on internal friction. This waste of energy and lack of focus makes the organisation less effective.

Creating a great atmosphere based on positive relationships, trust and mutual understanding is an essential leadership activity. So how do you achieve this? One thing that really helps is for people throughout the organisation to connect, to get to know each other and to understand each other's work.

Forming Connections

Leaders can initiate this by spending time working on the shopfloor or on the production line or whatever the frontline of their business is for a few hours or a day. This is not the same as the 'comfort worker' I described earlier who is avoiding their own leadership responsibilities. This is a disciplined and deliberate leadership activity to build connections and gather information. Doing this often is a good habit and other staff can move between teams for a day, or spend a day shadowing their boss. The aim is to build human connection and foster understanding.

The Leadership Book by Neil Jurd

"Creating a great atmosphere based on positive relationships, trust and mutual understanding is an essential leadership activity."

NJ

> **Example**
> *Alertacall, a fast-growing company in the UK, funds adventurous and developmental activities for staff to bring people from across the organisation together. So, groups from across the organisation can come together to learn art, or to go kayaking. The strong relationship formed in social activities carry back into the workplace and reduce friction between parts of the organisation.*

I suggest teams have regular meetings that focus on developing relationships, trust and mutual understanding. This could include a monthly or quarterly 'all staff' briefing, where senior leaders share what their issues are and take questions from the floor. This is a useful way of connecting different layers of a hierarchy. Where I have seen this work, the meeting has been run as an upbeat event: an engaging break from the normal with coffee and cakes provided. The aim is to make it inclusive and enjoyable, avoiding the corporate tendency to dull things down.

Alternatively, meetings could be organised conversations between small groups from across the business, the aim being to provide the time and the space to help the people in the room to get to know, trust and understand each other better. You could structure this, but there is no intent to solve anything in this meeting, just connect and create understanding. You might just ask people to talk about themselves as a person; their role in the company; the biggest thing they are working on now and how that makes them feel. And the group sizes need to be kept small, so the experience is not overwhelming for less socially confident team members, around 5 or 6 people in a meeting is about right.

While you have been reading this, you may have had some ideas of your own. Almost any activity that brings people from across the organisation together and allows them to get to know and understand each other will have a positive effect, which will help to develop a positive culture to allow the energy of the organisation to be focussed on great output instead of internal friction and competition.

> **Exercise**
>
> *Think about your current team. What could you do to develop better trust and mutual understanding?*

2.9 Levels of Communication

This chapter is about communicating and connecting with others, which are fundamental leadership skills. In my definition of leadership, which you will be familiar with by now, I stress the importance of leaders connecting with others.

Leaders achieve things far beyond what they could do alone, by engaging others intellectually and emotionally in pursuit of a clear and compelling purpose.

Engaging others to make that emotional and intellectual connection is an essential leadership skill. If we cannot engage others, we will not be able to lead them. The model at the heart of this idea comes from work by Father John Powell which presents the different levels of communication in a pyramid, with the lowest level of communication at the bottom, working to the highest level at the top.[18]

When I explain the model to groups, I introduce the idea that there is a level even lower than the bottom of the pyramid (I call this the Tomb) where people choose not to connect. In your working life this could be people in other departments that you are aware of, but have never greeted. The longer you leave it, the harder it gets.

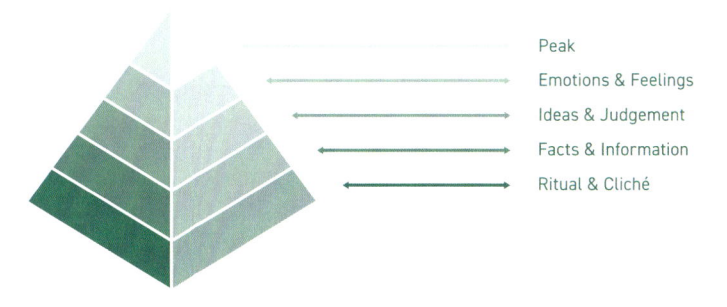

Peak
Emotions & Feelings
Ideas & Judgement
Facts & Information
Ritual & Cliché

Fig 7. Levels of Communication Pyramid, Father John Powell.

Above the tomb, and back to the actual model, the lowest level of communications is what we refer to as **Ritual and Cliché**. A version of this exists in all cultures; an exchange of greetings usually. In England, where I live, a typical exchange between two people would sound a bit like this:

'You, alright? Yes, I'm alright, are you alright?' 'Aye, better than the weather'. (I should explain at this point that in North Western England it rains a lot; the Lake District earns its name the hard way). In Sierra Leone in West Africa, where I once worked for a year, the greeting was a slightly more complex a list of enquiries: How's the body? The body's fine. How's the sleep? The sleep's fine. How's the family? The family's fine.

But this level of engagement is a shallow connection. When people greet each other in this way, if they are walking, they usually don't even slow down, and the tail end of the conversation will often be shouted over shoulders as people have passed. But that said, you must do this basic level of communication; if you ignore the ritual and cliché, you are considered rude. But do not confuse it for a meaningful connection in leadership terms. A ritual and cliché communication will not be enough to engage others in an idea.

The next level of communication is **Facts and Information**. Here people share things they know or have heard. A common example is people talking about tomorrow's weather, or the route they took to get to the office today, or some information about the new boss. But there is no opinion offered in this level of conversation. Frankly, conversation at this level is dull, and if it goes on too long your attention will drift. From a leadership point of view, you will not really engage people and form a connection at this level. Plans and instructions are something given at this level; information or orders are passed, but without any attempt to generate engagement.

Moving up another level we reach **Ideas and Judgements** – and at last, in connection terms we are getting somewhere. People are offering their perspective and some of their personality is entering the conversation. For instance, *'I think we should build more cycle lanes', 'education should be free for everyone', or 'working from home is better for family life'* are examples of Ideas and Judgements. And in leadership terms, expressing Ideas and Judgements can be an important part of connecting to people intellectually.

However, to really connect with people – to inspire them, to understand them, to build honest and open communications that create trust and mutual understanding, leaders need to be comfortable operating at the next level of the pyramid, which is **Emotions and Feelings**. The only way you know if your team is emotionally engaged and the only way to really get a feeling for what is going on in their minds, is to be able to talk at this level. When you express your own emotions and feelings to others, they will be engaged. If you talk in these terms, watch other peoples' body language; they will often lean in when you talk at this level.

And finally, at the very top of the pyramid – in high-performing relationships and teams, you reach **Peak** communications – which is where people just 'get' each other. They notice the subtlest signals, and a nod or a wink is enough to express a thought. This usually takes time to evolve and being able to work easily at an emotions and feelings level is essential for achieving Peak communications. People at this level will reach it by being able to talk openly and honestly about their feelings and emotions and will usually have a high number of shared values, although their backgrounds, beliefs and opinions can often be quite different.

Now you are aware of it, you will probably find yourself thinking more objectively about the quality of your engagement with other people. You'll find the further from the base of the pyramid you are, the better you connect and more rewarding the conversation is.

Part Two **People**

> *" There's only one thing I wish you to remember. If I say or do anything that hurts or vexes you, don't brood over it. Just out with it; and we shall come to an understanding at once"*

Henry Lawrence [19]

2.10 Developmental Conversations

In high-performing teams, there are open and honest communications, and it is natural for people to give each other performance related feedback. This is done to encourage and aid improvement and growth, so the team can achieve the best possible level of performance. Although conversations like this are sometimes seen as high-risk and best avoided, they are essential if the team is to be the best it can be. In low-performing teams these conversations rarely happen; instead, small problems are tolerated when they could easily be addressed. These conversations are not part of a disciplinary process; they are a normal part of team culture.

You need to have lots of positive development conversations. Positive comments and experiences usually have less impact than negative ones (we are programmed to scan for threat, which includes negative comments) so, to even the balance, people need to hear what they are doing well. Conversations like this will make people feel noticed, supported, and connected to you. They also lay the groundwork that makes it much easier for you to have corrective or improvement-focussed conversations when you need to.

The corrective or improvement focussed conversations are the ones that can sometimes seem daunting. But if you plan well whilst remaining calm and objective, then they will usually go well.

> **Example**
>
> *Laura was a senior leader in charge of adult training in a large voluntary youth organisation; she rarely turned up for events or meetings and was not carrying out her function effectively. Her boss, Peter, addressed the issue carefully, in line with the model suggested here. Laura's first response was relief; she explained that her day-job had become overwhelming and felt guilty about letting Peter and the other volunteers down. As a result of the discussion, Laura moved to a less demanding voluntary role in the organisation, and a volunteer with more spare time filled her post.*

A developmental conversation will usually be successful once you have made the point that you needed to, and the other person has taken ownership of the issue and agreed to resolve it. All this with the relationship intact and even strengthened.

This approach requires a structured conversation, for which I have designed a template which you can follow [20].

There are 5 stages to the developmental conversation model as follows: I'm going to expalin to you

- Connect and Establish
- Present and Evidence
- Pass Ownership
- Listen
- Confirm their Action

| Connect and Establish | Present and Evidence | Pass Ownership | Listen | Confirm their Action |

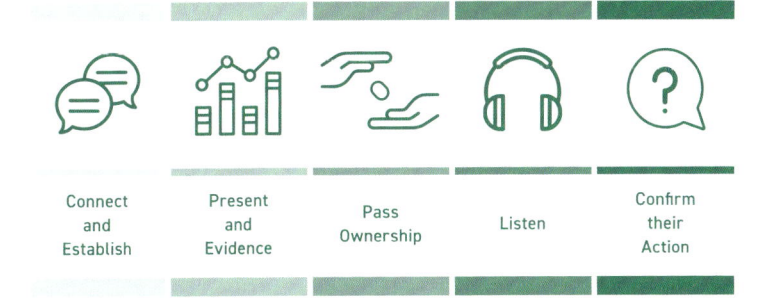

Fig 8. The Developmental Conversation Model.

Before anything

Preparation is critical to the success of this type of conversation. Make sure that you fully understand the situation and that you have checked the background facts. If you want to improve the way a team member focuses on detail, you need to understand and have to hand incidences where their grasp of the detail has led to problems.

If the issue is complex, it is usually worth making some notes regarding the facts for yourself, perhaps even rehearsing your part of the coming discussion.

Next, think about setting the right conditions for a successful meeting. Find a comfortable and non-threatening environment in which to have the conversation. Talking in a neutral meeting room is likely to lead to a better conversation than calling someone into your office. The aim is to allow the other person to focus on the issue you are discussing without stirring up a fear response in them, which might make them defensive and less open to changing or developing.

I will now explain each part of the process:

Connect and Establish

The first stage of this conversation is to Connect and Establish. Connect with the person and establish what the conversation is about. Start by thanking the other person for meeting with you and make them comfortable; perhaps offer them a drink. Set the tone for a relaxed and adult conversation.

Then quickly establish two things: what the conversation will be about; and what you think the person being interviewed brings to the team. I'll explain why in a moment.

You might say: *'Peter, I'd like us to chat about the way we onboard new recruits to the company. I know you lead this process, and I think that with your excellent attention to detail you have done a really good job modernising and improving the way it is structured and delivered'.*

So, from the outset, the other person knows the area under discussion and that they are well-regarded and that there is no personal threat to them. The scene is set for an adult conversation about doing things better, rather than a parent-child style interaction, which would usually be counter-productive.

Present and Evidence

Present in simple and non-threatening language what the issue is, and the improvement that needs to be achieved. At this stage, you should discourage interruption. Explain that you would like to set out the issue as you understand it, and that you would like to hear their response when you have finished.

The Present and Evidence stage could look like this: you might tell a member of your team that they received ten customer complaints last year, when the average number of complaints is two. This is clear and evidenced. You might then explain to them why customer complaints are damaging to your business and that you require them to receive significantly fewer complaints.

Whilst you are speaking, it is important to stay calm. The evidence will speak for itself; uncontrolled emotion can confuse and escalate the issue. The fact you have already set the conditions for a calm and adult conversation will really help; you are not making a personal attack, just presenting evidence and being clear that the situation must be rectified. If the other person interrupts, calmly ask them to let you finish explaining the issue. If they become angry or emotional, calmly wait for their emotion to pass, and then gently come back to where you were in explaining the issue.

Pass Ownership

Having presented the issue and the change that you need to see, you then pass ownership of the issue to the other person. People are more committed and energised by a solution which they have created for themselves but generally resistant to a solution which is imposed upon them.

At this stage, you only have your own perspective of the situation; the other person will understand what has been holding them back or impacting their performance. So, once you have defined the issue and the required standard of change, you allow the other person the autonomy to propose and own the solution. Handover the issue to them for them to consider and resolve. You have to resist the temptation to solve the problem for them. The power in this process comes from the other person taking ownership.

Staying with the customer complaints scenario, you might say:

'I would like to understand why there have been so many complaints, and what you will do to bring complaints about you below the company average'.

And remember, you are not telling the person off. There is no place for anger. This is all done calmly and objectively.

Part Two **People**

'*Hear them kindly and patiently, before gently bringing them back to telling you how they will resolve the issue.*'

NJ

Listen

Listen to them in a way that is present and open. The other person may offer information that changes the situation, but in most cases, just hear what they say. Give them space. They may reflect; they may express frustration or tell you things that you were not aware of. Whatever they say, usually the underlying facts are unchanged and you still need them to resolve the issue. Hear them kindly and patiently, before gently bringing them back to telling you how they will resolve the issue.

Confirm

The final stage of the conversation is for them to confirm what they have decided to do. Ask them to outline clearly what they propose to do and when this will happen. A great final question to gauge their commitment and mood is to ask: 'how do you feel about what you have decided to do?' This is an effective way of understanding the impact the conversation has had and usually you will be reassured that the conversation achieved the objective you hoped for. At this point, thank them sincerely for their time and see them out.

If you prepare well and follow this process - staying calm, kind, and present - it is likely that this type of conversation will go well and will help develop team performance. It may be helpful to explain the concept and process to your team upfront, so they are open to the idea of performance conversations and understand them to be supportive, rather than threatening.

Exercise

Can you think about a situation where the performance of an individual team member is holding back overall team performance? If so, try to use this model to sketch out a conversation you could have with that person to address the issue in a way that leaves them engaged and motivated.

Part Two **People**

'*The coach constructs an invisible and weightless framework to the conversation which helps move it towards a decision.*'

NJ

2.11 Developing Others – Coaching as a Leader

Coaching as a Leader

In high-performing teams, people are focussed on achieving the same clear and compelling purpose. Creativity is encouraged and people throughout the organisation are given freedom to work towards the purpose. It is important that leaders in high-performing teams allow and encourage this freedom and creativity throughout the organisation. It is energising and can be transformational.

Leaders who overly control others, by telling them what to do and by making sure that they, the leader, control all decision making and activity, reduce significantly the available brainpower and creativity available to the organisation. Coaching switches on all the brains and talent in the team, releasing senior leaders to think and focus on having a leadership effect.

As a leader, there is almost always no need to know the answer. Inexperienced and underconfident leaders often feel under pressure to demonstrate their value by offering answers, or they feel the need to exert authority by giving direction. Try to resist these temptations; **the more senior and influential a leader becomes, the less practical it is for them to know all the answers**, or to be involved in the detail of every decision.

As leaders, we have a role helping others find their own way of contributing towards the common purpose, which is where coaching comes in. Coaching is a supportive and empowering way for leaders to help their team members think through complex situations and make decisions. The person being coached retains ownership and autonomy of the issue. People are more inspired and energised following a plan they have decided for themselves, than something they have been ordered to do. A great deal of coaching is simply creating the time and space to think in a supportive environment.

The first thing to consider in a coaching conversation is to set the right conditions. Ideally, that means finding a location, free of distraction, where it is possible to focus completely on the issue you are considering. This could be a meeting room but could also mean going for a walk or sitting outside. Any environment without distractions is suitable. If the conversation is online, then agree to turn off notifications and other screens before you start.

The framework of coaching is very simple. Coaching is a structured conversation which follows a series of stages that allow a person to consciously make the right decision. The role of the coach is to create space, be curious and provide an invisible and weightless framework to the conversation which helps move it towards a decision.

There are plenty of models which you can use to structure a coaching conversation. I have developed one which I call the Coaching Cone, which is easy to follow. The roots of this are in the method of problem solving which I learned in the army, known as the Estimate, which effectively simplifies complexity. In the same way, the Coaching Cone takes a large volume of information and reduces it down to a simple decision.

There are various other coaching templates taught on coaching courses. Like the military Estimate, all coaching models are objective-orientated problem-solving techniques.

What is important is that adherence to the model does not interfere with the conversation. If the framework becomes a distraction, the quality of the conversation will be reduced.

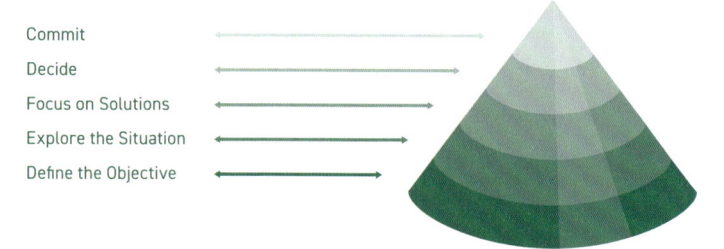

Commit
Decide
Focus on Solutions
Explore the Situation
Define the Objective

Fig 9. The Coaching Cone by Neil Jurd

The Coaching Cone

Any coaching session starts with clarifying what the objective of the coaching conversation is.

Step 1. Define the Objective

Coaching conversations are often required because people express frustration or a feeling of confusion, and they usually need some help untangling the important information from everything else that is going on. The first role of the coach is to provide some focus to the conversation, and the way to do this is to define the objective.

The sorts of questions you could ask to help you do this could include:

- What is it you are trying to solve?
- What is the real issue for you here?
- What are you trying to achieve?
- What would we have solved for this to be an effective use of our time?
- Are there any similar issues in your life?

Often there is a difference between the 'presenting issue', which might be superficial, and the 'real' or underlying issue that is more substantial. A presenting issue could be a particular relationship with their boss, but the real issue might be that the person has trust issues and struggles to form relationships. This first step of the process takes patience; superficial issues are often easy to solve, but it is far more useful to identify and work with the more substantial underlying cause.

Superficial issues include	Underlying issues include
· Issues with the boss	· Lack of direction and purpose
· Time management	· Identity and sexuality
· An underperforming employee	· Fear (often of failure)
· A frustrating project	· Imposter syndrome
	· Lack of recognition

You may need to work through the superficial issues to get to the underlying ones. Finding the right focus for the conversation will underwrite the value of what follows.

Step 2. Explore the Situation

In this second step we help the other person to make sense of what is actually going on. Calmly and gently, encouraging them to think objectively and logically, we help them to unpick the truth of what they are dealing with. Often, there are huge breakthroughs at this stage, as rational thinking is gently and kindly applied to situations which might have previously been charged with emotion.

Exploring the situation can separate the fact from the overwhelming fiction, identifying the important parts of a problem.

Questions at this stage might be:

- What is the current situation?
- How would other people see this?
- What are the three most important facts?
- How serious is this?
- What makes you think that?

You can keep the person focussed with a few simple questions such as:

- Is there more?
- What else?

There are hundreds of variations of these questions; the main thing for a coach at this stage is to be gently curious and allow the person being coached the time and space to think. Silence is important; as a leader in the coaching role, allow silence and resist the temptation to step in and offer solutions.

Step 3. Focus on Solutions

Here the conversation shifts from talking about the problem to talking about the solution. It is as if the weightless framework just tilts slightly on its axis, encouraging the person you are coaching to reflect and think their way out of the situation. People often enjoy - or at least are compelled to - focus on the drama and rights and wrongs of a situation. The human fascination with drama explains why soap operas are so popular, however, there are no solutions in the drama, so the coach must move the conversation away from Coronation Street and focus on solutions.

This is the part of the process which I think of as the move from 'interesting' to 'useful'. The aim is to encourage the other person's brain to start exploring possible solutions. The first two stages have allowed the other person to understand things much more clearly than they did before, so often, this stage is surprisingly easy. The conversation may move here naturally and without a nudge. If that happens, allow it. Skillful coaches are often silent.

Something I learned from military planning in the army is the idea of having to think of and develop several workable solutions before deciding which one is best.

Questions you might ask at this stage include:

- What might work?
- What have you thought of trying?
- What else could you try?
- If money were not an issue, what would you do?
- If people were not an issue, what would you do?
- What does your instinct tell you?

And again, you can keep the person you are coaching in the spotlight and doing the thinking with what I call 'add on questions' or prompts such as:

- Tell me more
- What else?

These 'add on questions' work surprisingly well, often opening a whole new area and taking the conversation to a more substantial seam of richness. This is the coaching equivalent of when you try to checkout with your online grocery shopping, and the app asks 'is there something you forgot'?

As a coach, really listen to and watch the other person. Their voice and body language will often give you clear indications of how they feel about the different options they envision. They will be more positive when they talk about the options which they are most excited by, and they will be subdued when they describe the ones that they find less satisfactory. As before, stay in the coaching role and resist the temptation to give them direction or opinion about which solution is the right one. If you do, then the entire process becomes an artificial construction to help them guess what you wanted them to do all along.

By the end of this stage you are aiming to have at least two, ideally more possible solutions to work with.

Step 4. Decision

The next stage is to review the possible solutions, and to make a decision. By this stage, there might be a clear and obvious preferred way forward in which case the decision will be simple, or there could still be several options available in which case you will explore these options to find the best solution.

Often, all that the coach needs to do is ask a simple question. Ones that might work are:

- What is your decision?
- Which option do you like best?
- Which one of these options best meets your objective?
- Do you know what you are going to do?

It is then helpful to bring the plan to life; ask the person to describe how they are going to carry out the plan, who will be involved, and when.

Step 5. Action

Once the person has decided what they are going to do, your role as a coach is to help them to commit to turning their decision into action.

Questions that explore this are:

- How certain are you to follow through on the decision you have just made?
- On a scale of 1 to 10 how committed are you to the decision you have just made?

And finally:

- Talk me through what you will do and when?

Remember, your aim here is not to make them commit to their plan, you are just checking their own commitment to that plan. Because if they are not genuinely committed themselves, their decision will usually not lead to effective action.

The result of a successful coaching process is a plan that the other person has calmly and logically made and committed to see through. And you, as their leader, will have struck the right balance between providing clear support and ensuring the other person feels empowered. You have avoided the strong temptation to 'step in' and show you know the answers; instead, you have allowed them to think and create a way forward which they will own and feel enthused by.

Reflection

- Have there been occasions recently when you could have applied a coaching rather than directive style of leadership?
- How and when could you bring coaching into your leadership style?

2.12 Developing Others – The Performance Equation

In this section, I will introduce you to The Performance Equation: a simple and useful piece of theory which helps individuals and teams to perform to the upper limits of their potential. I found this model in Timothy Gallwey's book, The Inner Game of Work[21]. While the model has its roots in tennis coaching, it applies in work as well as it does in sport.

As a leader, by engaging others we achieve things far beyond what we can achieve on our own. Therefore, helping others to achieve their best and to come together in order to work effectively is an important aspect of leadership. In the ideal team, everyone would be excellent in their own role. Then they would fit effortlessly into a team of similarly excellent others, who work well together and are focussed on achieving the same objective. These would be people at their best: working together to build a team which was greater than the sum of its constituent parts - as good as it could be.

I once spoke at the same event as the former England Rugby coach, Sir Clive Woodward, on an ocean liner which had been booked for networking. I was quite a bit further down the bill than him. He delivered his talk and was helicoptered off the boat (when that happens, you have made it as a speaker). I was not given the helicopter option, but I did spend several very lovely nights in a first-class cabin which I didn't have to pay for, and I met some great people. One of the themes I remember from Sir Clive's talk was that he viewed team performance in these same terms; each team member had to be their best, and then the team had to come together excellently. These were two essential aspects of creating a great team.

This level of peak performance in individuals and teams is rare. Often, teams that in theory should be excellent and which bring together high-performing experts, do not perform well. The same is true of individuals. Talented people with strong CVs sometimes do not deliver to expectations. This model will help you to understand why that happens and allow you to focus effort on enabling stronger performance.

The model, which is simple to the point of perfection is this:

$$P = p - i$$

Performance = potential - interference

Fig 10. The Performance Equation, Timothy Gallwey

I'll explain what the 3 elements of the model are:

- Our **Performance** is our output. This is what actually happens: whether we get our work done; score goals; sing a solo beautifully; or, in this case, lead the team effectively.
- Our **Potential** is the very best that we could possibly be, if all of our talents were perfectly applied.
- **Interference** is whatever can get in the way and puts us off.

This idea of interference is very similar to something which Clausewitz defined in his book 'On War' early in the 19th Century, where he identified the concept of 'friction' in war; friction being the force that can undermine a good plan with unexpected chaos.

> **Interference**
> *A few years ago Monty worked in Glasgow in a job he was well qualified for. He weekly commuted to this job, with his family living 150 miles further south in Preston. During the week Monty lived in a ground floor flat paid for by his company. The flat was in a rough part of the city situated on a church square which after dark was frequented by noisy drunks. His weekly commute to and from Preston was frequently delayed, usually on the way to work on Monday morning, often making him late. The building he worked in was airless (the windows were designed so they could not be opened), the working culture was one of process and 'busyness' and he had a fraught relationship with his direct boss; above him was a man who often gave him work last thing on Friday which needed to be finished by Monday lunchtime. After a year Monty resigned from this role. In theory, Monty should have thrived in this job, but there was so much interference around the edges of the job that he found himself unhappy and unable to fulfil his potential.*
>
> *Think about how interference might be impacting on your performance, or that of workmates and team members.*

To Perform well, we need to maximise Potential and minimise Interference.

Maximising Potential

At the individual level, this is about having the right skills so you are as well prepared for the task in hand as possible. That is likely to mean study and practice. At the team level, team potential rests on two things: first, the individual potential of each team member, so everybody in the team has to work to develop their own potential. Second, the potential of the overall team, meaning that when the team members are brought together, between them they bring the right skills for team success. Good selection and training of team members contributes to this.

Minimising Interference

However high the potential is, there will always be interference. Within teams, frustrations and irritations are often tolerated and allowed to simmer, rather than being addressed. Or there is a culture in which constructive criticism is not welcome and confronting interference might not be encouraged. Unchecked and sometimes hidden interference can undermine individual and team performance.

Having the right organisational culture is essential in being able to address interference. In organisations where people are clearly focussed on a clear and compelling purpose, there is less interference. Having a culture of trust and mutual understanding characterised by open and honest communications within the team makes it okay to express doubts and offer constructive criticism. Individuals also need to have that same ability to be honest about their own internal interference and be willing to address it.

Interference is usually so damaging because it is not exposed or diagnosed; it tends to sit just below the surface, kept there by cultural taboos and fear of confrontation. To resolve it in order to allow improvement, interference must be brought into the open and dealt with. Coaching and team development can be extremely helpful for this: encouraging an individual or a team to reflect on what is holding them back and then act to resolve it. Individually, or as a team, be willing to stop and ask the right questions from time to time. Those questions are likely to be simple and to the point; try 'what is interfering with our performance, and what can we do to reduce that interference'?

Reflection

List two things which cause you interference?

1. ....

2. ....

List one thing you can do to increase your potential?

1. ....

Part Two **People**

'*Having a culture of trust and mutual understanding characterised by open and honest communications within the team makes it okay to express doubts and offer constructive criticism.*'

NJ

2.13 Understanding Yourself – Input, Process and Output

Effective leaders know themselves well and work hard to understand and control their emotions, so that their effect on people and events is positive. The opposite of this is the emotionally reactive leader that people approach with caution, whose uncontrolled emotional highs and lows set the tone for the organisation. This sort of leader generates fear and uncertainty.

To be an effective leader and to create an environment in which there is trust and people feel safe, being able to understand and control our own emotions and feelings is essential.

The model below[22] is one which I have created to help you visualise this concept. Like most of the models I have designed, it came out of a coaching session, where I sketched it to help capture what was going on for the client. This slightly evolved version of the original sketch links to some of the other ideas in this book.

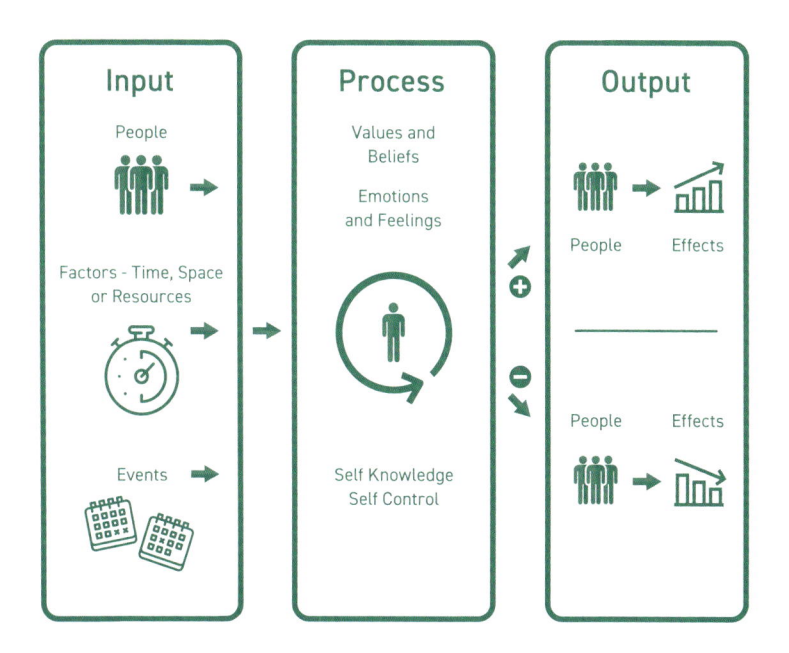

Fig 11. Image showing the Input, Process and Output of how to have a positive effect on people you lead.

There are three stages to the model. First, the 'Input': the things that happen to the leader. Second, the 'Process', which is how the leader handles the things that happen to them; and third, the 'Output', which is how the leader impacts others. With a leader who is not in control of their emotions and feelings, the flow from input to output is uninterrupted. If the leader has experienced negativity, this is passed on to their team. This will have a detrimental impact on them and their output and they in turn might well pass the negativity on.

INPUT

This is the raw material of things that happen to us. I break this down into three inputs: People, Factors and Events.

People

People are having an effect on us all the time; they might praise us or shout at us, they might show approval, withhold love, or send a text that excites you or leaves you confused. Perhaps your boss has demanded you rewrite a document for the Board. Or perhaps the same boss wants to give you a performance bonus. People can generate a lot of complex inputs.

Factors

Factors include time, space and resources. There might be a deadline looming, or maybe you have all the time you need. Maybe your organisation needs more space or is in the wrong space. Then resources: do you have enough money? Does your IT work? And is your team the right size? You will probably be able to think of factors that apply in your own working life right now.

Events

Events might include congestion on the way to work, sunny weather, the coffee machine breaking, you winning first prize in a raffle, or the global outbreak of a virus.

PROCESS

The next stage of the model is 'Process', which is how we handle the input. Any two people would be likely to respond differently to the same input. This is because we all see the world slightly differently. Our unique life experiences shape our values and beliefs while our values and beliefs shape our emotions and feelings. These things influence how we process input.

If we value fairness and inclusion, we will have an emotional response to obvious unfairness. We might feel furious, helpless, or frustrated. If we believe ourselves to be a competent leader, we might respond well to constructive criticism because we know it is not a threat to us. We feel secure and able to develop.

When we become overwhelmed by input, it is easy to respond mindlessly and automatically. If the input was negative, we might become defensive, or sarcastic or withdraw. If the input was positive, then we might become over-confident and make poor decisions. So, to be an effective leader, we need to be able to control our emotional response to input before we engage with other people.

Usually the key to doing this well is to remove yourself from pressure and to create the time and space to think. If time allows, coaching can be very helpful. But, in most situations, just finding a quiet space and taking a few moments or minutes to put things in perspective is sufficient.

OUTPUT

Output is the effect the leader has on others. I use the definition that *Leaders achieve things far beyond what they could do alone, by engaging others intellectually and emotionally in pursuit of a clear and compelling purpose.* Consequently, effective leaders have their output through other people and those 'other' people have a wider effect working towards whatever we are trying to achieve.

If we have gone through the 'Process' stage well, by which I mean mindfully and understanding and controlling our own emotions, then our output is likely to be positive. Our effect on others will be positive and their effect on the world will be positive. Effective leaders are stable and consistent and the people that work for them feel safe and supported.

If you can apply this model in your own leadership practice, it will help you to provide the stability, trust and consistency that brings out the best in people, so they can concentrate on having a positive effect in the world.

Reflection

Over the course of a day, try to be conscious of how this model applies to you. What inputs do you experience, how do you process them, and what are your positive and negative outputs?

2.14 Understanding People – The Foundations Model

In this section, I am going to introduce you to the Foundations Model, which is a useful way of helping you to understand some of the personal factors that enable or limit your own and others' performance. I have created this model as a way of showing the importance of what lies beneath the surface in sustaining what is seen above. **Effective leadership performance can only be built on solid foundations.**

If you are distracted by personal issues, then your performance will suffer. Conversely, if you are in the best possible health and feeling mentally resilient, then you will be at your most effective as a leader. Understanding this concept is useful, both to help you to focus on improving your own performance and to allow you to better understand and support the people in your team.

The Foundations Model [23] is a simple way of visualising this concept.

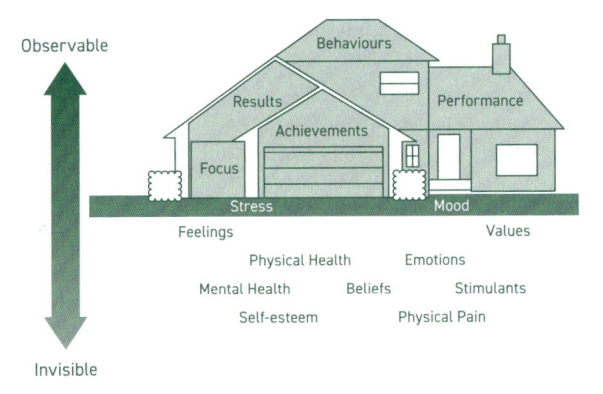

Fig 13. Image showing The Foundations Model

When we look at human performance it is like a house, we see the construction, but not the foundations. So above ground level we see a few things: we see people's results, achievements or failures and we see how they are working. Then, a little less obviously, we might notice how they are performing and behaving. How able they are to focus and how consistent their performance is. Depending on how hard we look, closer to the ground, we might be able to see their mood and their level of stress, or these things might be kept out of sight.

What is less obvious is what is going on in the foundations of the model. Obviously in a building, the foundations are an essential part of the construction, but they are usually not visible from the outside. If they are strong, the building they support is strong. If they are shaky, then so is the building.

In the foundations are our emotions and feelings and our values and beliefs. We might sometimes choose to share these, or a skilled and interested observer might be able to interpret them. Unfortunately, in many working cultures, it can be considered 'unprofessional' to talk about these things.

Staying below the ground, issues such as self-esteem and mental health will have an impact on a person's effectiveness, but these are often deliberately concealed from others. Performance can, of course, be influenced by physical pain, which is usually not visible but can be distracting and potentially very limiting.

As a leader, you need to know that what is going on in the foundations has an impact on how a person performs. You need to understand and challenge whatever is in your own foundations and be willing and able to support others at this level. Being able to work at this level - below ground level, if you like - is an important aspect of creating both a feeling of safety in the team and a culture based on trust, mutual understanding, strong relationships and honest communications.

To support someone in this way, just make the time to connect; ask them how they are and really listen to their answer. Then think about how you can support them to help them create steady foundations to work from.

PART THREE

LEADING TEAMS AND ORGANISATIONS

THIS SECTION WILL HELP YOU TO PLAN, MAKE DECISIONS, FOCUS EFFORT, AND DEVELOP A POSITIVE TEAM CULTURE

3.1 Define and Share your Style and Vision Early

Leaders deliver most of their effect through other people by connecting and engaging with them in pursuit of a clear and compelling purpose. To do this effectively, the leader must have a positive impact on the people they lead.

Generally, people feel uncomfortable with uncertainty. The more clarity and reassurance a leader can give to the team, the better. Effective leaders create a sense of safety for their team. The more information and inspiration a leader can give to their team, the safer those people feel, and the more able they are to use their initiative and make good decisions. People do not like or trust detached leaders, and a lack of communication and clarity will lead to mistrust and a poor working culture. There is a real imperative for leaders who want to build and maintain a positive culture to work hard to inspire and be understood.

As a leader, giving people clarity and reassurance about who you are and how you work creates safety and has a positive impact. You will have your own style and preferences, so it really helps other people if they understand how you like to work, and the culture that you are looking to grow. This goes a long way towards preventing misunderstanding and frustration. The better people know and understand you as a leader, the more freedom you will be able to give them and the more initiative they will be able to take.

Who you are and how you work

There is a simple structure that I suggest you use to define who you are and how you work. First, begin by writing a paragraph that will introduce you at a personal level. The more you can share about yourself, the better. Only share things that will encourage connection and allow people to feel comfortable.

Whilst being so open might feel unnatural or uncomfortable, effective leadership is based on personal connection, not positional power; this openness and honesty will help to form the connection and understanding which will allow you to engage others and get the best from them. Teams thrive on human connection.

Start by writing a paragraph that introduces you on a personal level. As long as you are sharing things that will encourage connection and allow people to feel comfortable. Where are you from? What sort of family do you have? What do you enjoy? What matters to you? What do you value in the world? What are your hobbies and interests? The aim of this is to help create personal connection.

Then explain your working style. Establish how you would like things to be (otherwise you will quickly become sucked into accepting the way things are). What sort of culture do you want to work in? How do you want your team to feel? How will people communicate? How important is honesty? Do you value face to face meetings? What is your view on being copied in on messages and being kept 'in the loop?' (Personally, I think being kept in too many loops distracts leaders from leading). Can people book you to attend meetings? What level of detail do you want to be engaged in; what matters to you?

As soon as you are ready, pull people together and present this work to them. Find a nice venue, offer refreshments, and present this in an informal chat. Be yourself, not your appointment, and use this occasion to connect with your team and reassure. If you can get this right you will have gone a long way towards creating the conditions for a positive culture.

People need to feel Connected to the Purpose

As a leader, you need to think about and then share what the Clear and Compelling Purpose is, as well as your vision of how you will work towards that purpose. Knowing what is going on and feeling part of the bigger picture is a powerful motivator; conversely, a feeling of disconnection is demoralising. Often the aspirations of organisations are captured and then concealed in turgid five-year plans that are rarely seen by most staff.

On our leadership courses, we run learning projects that are designed to make some members of the team feel disconnected from the purpose, and their feedback after the exercise is always negative. This replicates the reality in many organisations, where the staff on the ground have little or no understanding of what the senior leaders are trying to achieve; without knowing that, it is hard for them to innovate and contribute.

Define and Share your Clear and Compelling Purpose and Vision

Start by making sure you are clear what your purpose is and, if it was set a while ago, that it is still relevant. Once you have clarified what your purpose is, try to sketch out a rough vision of the journey you will take in moving towards that purpose and what success will look like. Think about what route you are planning to take to move the team from where you are to where you are going and what people can expect to experience on that journey. This should not be a detailed business plan, but it needs to be enough to clarify your thinking and allow other people to understand where you will be leading them.

When people are learning to be mountain leaders or ski guides, they are taught to brief groups in this way. Giving them a sense of the next leg of the journey, what challenges they might face, and what the destination will look like. This allows the group to feel connected to the process, to prepare well, make suggestions and better support the leader and other group members.

When you are clear about your team's purpose and journey, share your message widely and often. I suggest getting people together and presenting these ideas to everyone, as well as sharing these ideas in smaller groups and individual conversations. What your team is trying to achieve, how you plan to get there, and what success will look like are all things that should be well known, well understood and should be a clear, regular theme running through all your messages. Your team will be happy to have a clear sense of your ideas and where you hope to lead them.

These ideas are all about helping the team to feel comfortable and safe with you as a leader. The better that your team understands your thinking and priorities, the more they will be able to make the right decisions and take action on your behalf. These ideas can either be applied when you are already established in a leadership position, or when you are taking up a new appointment.

> **Exercise**
>
> *Try to bring to life the suggestions in this section by writing about your personality, way of working and helping others to understand where their work will be focussed.*
>
> - *First, write a short and simple document (a single page of A4 should be plenty) about yourself, your working style and the culture you hope to build.*
> - *Then on your own or with others, clarify the Clear and Compelling Purpose of your team and sketch out how you plan to achieve it.*

3.2 Mission Command – Why Napoleon Did Not Meddle

In this section, I am going to talk about a leadership culture and style of working which is called Mission Command[24]. Mission Command has its roots in a study of battles in the Napoleonic wars and is now practised by (or at least is taught to) most modern military forces. I learned about Mission Command as a cadet at Sandhurst, and continued to learn about it and apply it throughout my time in the army and then I applied it when I led logistics for British Sugar.

The concept originated from a study by Carl Von Clausewitz into Napoleon's defeat of the Prussian Army early in the 19th Century. The defeated Prussian Army was highly controlled, bureaucratic and status conscious. There was very tight discipline and officers were expected to follow orders. On the other hand, Napoleon focussed on inspiring his soldiers and empowering his leaders. He actively encouraged his officers to understand the big picture and to make decisions in battle without checking with him. Napoleon's leadership style was the essence of what is now called Mission Command.

Mission Command worked for Napoleon right up to Moscow and, more usefully for the reader, I have seen it successfully applied in a range of organisations including businesses, schools, universities, and charities. It allows leaders to harness the enthusiasm and talent of others. It is energising and empowering, allows speedy decision-making, and helps people to prioritise and to focus on the important work.

Mission Command is largely about culture: it insists on certain positive ways of working, and all activity is focussed on a clear and robust aim. I have captured the essence of Mission Command in this simple Model:

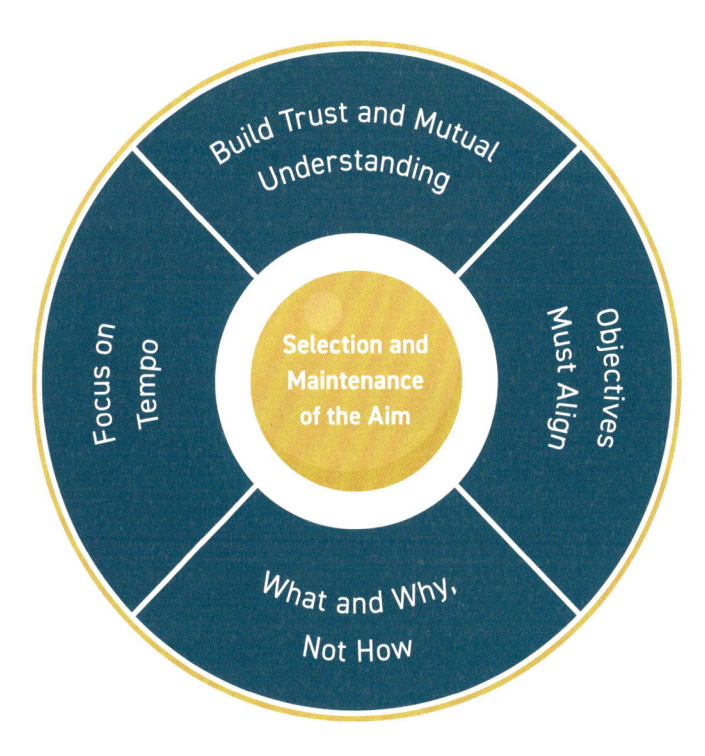

Fig 14. Image showing the elements of Mission Command.

Selection and Maintenance of the Aim is the core principle of Mission Command, around which everything is built. In this book and in my work, I use the term 'Clear and Compelling Purpose' to mean the same thing.

When organisations are not clear what they are trying to achieve, there is internal friction and competition, and the organisation lacks purpose. Defining the right aim excites people and gives them something to work towards. 'Maintaining' the aim means that the leader needs to make sure that the aim is still relevant.

> **The Importance of Aim**
>
> In recent years, the military campaigns in Iraq and Afghanistan both suffered strategic ambiguity: that is, they lacked a clear aim. Before that the US engagement in Vietnam was much the same; there was a disconnect between the objectives of politicians and the US military, with disastrous consequences.

Around this all-important aim, Mission Command insists on a positive culture which includes:

Build Trust and Mutual Understanding

Internal competition, gossip and friction are discouraged, and different parts of an organisation are expected to support and work with each other in pursuit of the overall Aim. Leaders are not allowed to interfere or micromanage, but instead they train and empower subordinates and trust them to do their best. Mutual Understanding is encouraged by sharing information and encouraging connections throughout the organisation. This allows departments to better support each other. Trust is fundamental to allowing leaders at all levels to make timely decisions on behalf of the organisation without referring decisions upwards for approval.

Objectives Within the Organisation Must Align

When the internal objectives of an organisation are properly aligned, everybody is clearly working towards the same thing; the energy of the organisation is connected and focussed. The objectives of each team member should feed into and support the objectives of the person they report to. Everybody's work clearly contributes tot he overall aim of the organisation. When objectives are aligned in this way, team members at the lowest level feel a sense of purpose; they see the big picture and understand how their work supports the organisation's strategic aim.

An important aspect of this is that everybody clearly understands what the person they report to is trying to achieve, which allows them to use their initiative and creativity to support that. This is energising, and it engages and empowers people.

When direction is given leaders are told WHAT to achieve, and WHY, but not HOW.

The What is a simple and easily understood statement, and the Why gives the reason and purpose that helps to motivate people by creating an emotional connection to the task. But allowing people to work out the How for themselves is important. Leaders at every level are trusted to create their own plan and given as much freedom as possible. The role of the senior leader is to support and resource and potentially even coach the person who has been given the task, but not to meddle or direct. This means that people feel ownership of their part of the plan, and it frees senior leadership to focus on more strategic work. By being allowed to create their own How, leaders at all levels are encouraged to think creatively and develop the plans which they will themselves carry out. Usually these plans will be better linked to reality than plans created by people further away from the situation.

Tempo

Mission Command involves making effective decisions quickly and turning them into action. In Mission Command this is called Tempo. Leaders at every level are expected to have the knowledge and the confidence to make decisions, rather than passing decision making upwards to more senior people or committees. The Mission Command way of working makes Tempo possible, because everybody is focussed on the same objective, and the culture of Trust and Understanding allows senior leaders to trust their team to make decisions on their behalf.

Summary

The Mission Command environment mirrors the Excel phase of the model of team development in this book. Like the Excel stage of team development, a true Mission Command environment is hard to achieve and harder to maintain. Gossip and internal competition tend to undermine trust and mutual understanding, and people lose sight of the aim they should be working towards as process and procedure take precedence over purpose.

It takes leadership, focused effort, and training to build a Mission Command culture. Thinking and decision making are delegated to leaders at all levels, anchored by a clear and well understood aim. When Mission Command is applied well, the culture will be creative, agile and energetic and there will be an absence of internal friction.

The challenge for a leader is to create a Mission Command environment, and then to be brave enough to let it run. Allowing that there may sometimes be some minor errors, but the benefits in pace and energy will outweigh the risk associated with tactical errors. Most leaders lose their nerve and grip the detail, but leaders who can work in this way maximise their own leadership effect by enabling others.

Reflection

Are there aspects of Mission Command that you can apply in your leadership practice? If so, can you list up to 3 concrete changes in line with this concept?

1.
....
2.
....
3.
....

3.3 The Importance of Diversity and Inclusion

If you want to build an excellent team, it will be diverse. Diversity of background, education, race, social connections, gender, sexuality, outside interests and almost any other way you can think of brings a richness of experience. There is no correlation between talent or potential on one hand, and race, sexuality, religion, or professional ability on the other. High IQs, emotional intelligence, great work ethics, creativity and commitment can be found in all quarters of society.

Teams where people are too similar limit their own potential. It is a form of organisational in-breeding. In teams like this thinking will be less radical because it will be based on a narrower breadth of experience. Similar educations, lifestyles and hobbies limit the gene pool of creativity. Inherited social conventions encourage status, hierarchy, and a tendency to conform. Too many people have ideas that overlap. A team of similar people won't know what they don't know.

In high performing teams, positive difference is encouraged. Diverse backgrounds and beliefs can provide the backdrop for a creative and vibrant culture. Different experiences, upbringing, perspectives and beliefs within a team can provide a rich environment for creativity and thinking. However, cognitive biases, which are ideas imprinted on us from an early age, usually make us prefer people who remind us of ourselves. It is human nature to form groups - tribes if you like - in which we feel safe, and to be suspicious or fearful of people who are not members of our tribe.

To give you an example of this, the 'Brown Eyes Blue Eyes' experiment[25] carried out with 8-year-old students in a US primary school in 1968 saw students with blue eyes easily turned against students with brown eyes. It took the class teacher minutes to achieve this. The students easily believed that those with the other eye colour were inferior to those with their own eye colour.

Part Three **Leading Teams and Organisations**

'Teams where people are too similar limit their own potential. It is a form of organisational in-breeding.'

NJ

The tendency to trust people like ourselves whilst rejecting those who are different is very deeply rooted. In pre-historic time, this behaviour was a useful programming, as anybody that was not part of our own tribe was, potentially, a threat. But in the multicultural times we live and work in this programming is unhelpful and irrelevant; good leaders work hard to create inclusive organisational cultures, built on trust and mutual understanding. However, to build high-performing diverse and inclusive teams, we need to overcome our own unconscious bias.

Reflective Exercise:

- Does your team or organisation tend to recruit a certain type of person?
- Can you see a downside to this approach?
- What could you do differently?

Space for your answers:

3.4 Focusing Effort

Leaders and teams should be focused on the most impactful and relevant work. Earlier in this book I explained the importance of Clear and Compelling Purpose. I have also outlined the Mission Command way of working, which emphasises the importance of objectives being aligned.

In many organisations, however, people are not focussed on the same Clear and Compelling Purpose, so their effort is diluted. Often, it goes unnoticed, because they seem to be going broadly in the right direction; they are not contributing to the purpose, but it is not so obvious that it stands out. Consequently, their irrelevant activity tends to be tolerated.

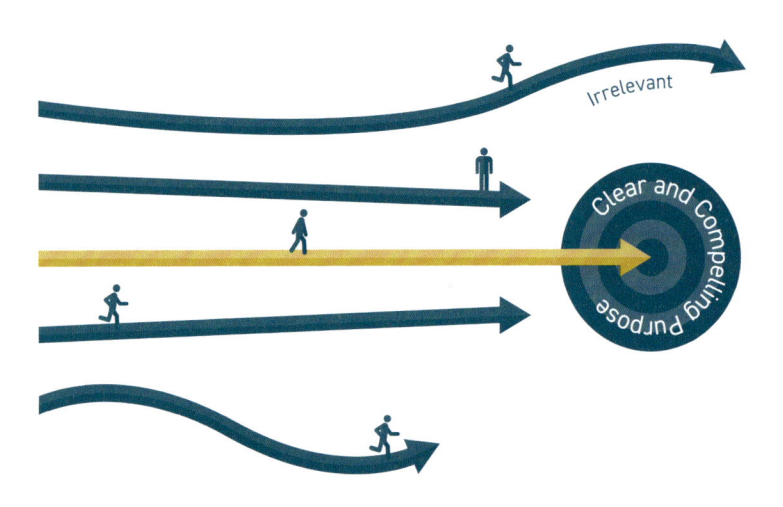

Fig 15. Focusing effort on Clear and Compelling Purpose.

There are many reasons for this – misunderstanding; different ideas about what is important; or internal competition. Sometimes people will concentrate on easy work, or high-profile work that they think is good for their own career profile. The result can be an organisation in which people are working, sometimes extremely hard, on things that do not help to take the organisation where it is trying to go.

If activity cannot be linked to the Clear and Compelling Purpose, then either the activity is wrong, or the purpose is wrong. This is not something you can ignore, because people are using time and resources to do work that is not useful.

A few years ago, I was in a coaching session with a client who worked for a national charity. She was frustrated by a member of her management team whose work was high profile and impactful, but often not useful for the organisation he was part of. He worked hard enough, but his boss did not consider his work to be particularly useful. During that coaching session, we sketched out the framework for the idea I outline here and, since then, several of my clients have used this idea and found it very effective.

Part Three **Leading Teams and Organisations**

One way to help focus on what is important, is to ask people or departments to name their top three projects. Then, compare those projects against the clear and compelling purpose. Award a score out of 10 for the potential impact of each project, and a further score out of 10 for the relevance of that project to the overall Clear and Compelling Purpose. Then multiply one score by the other – which will generate a total of between 0 and 100.

Using this scoring method, a high impact project that is highly relevant to the clear and compelling purpose could score 100 points, whilst a high impact but irrelevant project might score 10/100. Relevant but low-impact projects would also score lowly. Only impactful and relevant projects score well.

The aim would be for everyone in the team and every department in the organisation to be focussed on work that scored highly against these simple criteria.

If you were running a team planning day, you could bring this to life by using a scoring target with concentric rings and letting parts of your team score and place their own work on the target. And you could encourage teams and leaders to challenge each other's thinking with different teams scoring each other's projects. Beyond helping to focus work where it is most important, this also enables people to understand what their counterparts in other teams are working on.

Reflective Exercise

Think of 3 ongoing projects that your team are working on. Follow the explanation above to award each project a score using the table below.

Project	Impact	Relevance	Total / 100
EXPO 22	8	2	16
1.			
2.			
3.			

3.5 Making Decisions - The OODA Loop [26]

Napoleon once said that 'nothing is more difficult, and therefore more precious, than to be able to decide' [27]

That is as true today as it was when he said it, as technology develops rapidly, and information moves instantly and in huge volume. Modern leaders can find themselves frozen in the glare of too much information or missing a critical decision point because they are waiting for even more information to become available. In high-performing teams people make decisions quickly and effectively.

A useful model to help understand decision making is called the OODA loop, also called the 'Boyd cycle'. It was created by United States Air Force Colonel John Boyd, who was training fighter pilots to defeat the enemy in aerial combat: an environment where fast and accurate decision making is essential. The OODA loop is a simple and effective tool to help organisations make the right decisions at the right speed.

Although values and beliefs do not feature in the original OODA loop, I have added them in based on my own observations. Our values and beliefs shape everything we notice, everything we decide and everything we do, so I have put them at the heart of this model.

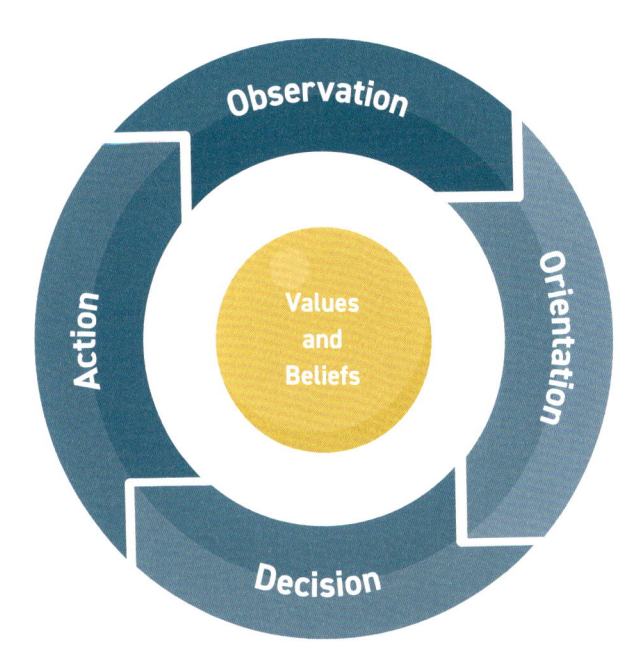

Fig 16. OODA Loop, Col. John Boyd USAF.

Observation

This is the first essential step to making effective and timely decisions. People and organisations must be able and willing to look up from whatever task they are focussed on and notice what is going on around them, both in their business and in the wider world. By doing this, by observing, they notice changes. For instance, changes to the environment, cultural changes, changes to the market and changes to the law. The sorts of activities that help with this include keeping up to date with world news and trade publications, continuous professional development, recruiting new staff with different experiences, and attending seminars. The Observation stage of the OODA loop is about being open to information.

Orientation

This is where we interpret what we noticed in the Observation stage of the model. We think about what we have seen, read, or been told and we consider whether and how it affects us. To do this successfully, it has to be a cultural 'norm' to take time to think. Often, in organisations being busy and being present are expected, and thinking is a discouraged luxury. Sometimes decisiveness is overrated, with poor decisions being preferred to slower but better considered ones.

Decision

Moving to Decide is a conscious step, which some teams and organisations struggle with; instead, they become stuck Observing and Orientating. They Observe, they Orientate, then they Observe some more, they Orientate some more, but nothing happens; I call this getting stuck on the OOOO line, instead of going round the OODA loop, because they do not move onto the third step in this process and Decide. That could be a decision to do nothing – but the decision to do nothing is made consciously and deliberately.

> **Example**
> *I was once involved in a planning situation when I was involved in running a summer camp for 400 young people. We knew severe weather was coming, but the planning team struggled to make the difficult decision to bring the young people into safety before the storm hit. I have reflected on this since and think that a combination of factors led to this example of decision-constipation; the group had some internal friction and there was a clear hierarchy which may have led junior members of the planning team to hold back with their opinions and concerns.*

Action

Once a decision has been made, in needs to be translated into Action. If the OODA process has been followed, it is likely to be the right Action. Logical and based on the best information.

Things go wrong when stages in the OODA loop have been missed. Some leaders and organisations tend to make decisions without first Observing and Orientating. The resulting decisions are usually flawed. Others fail to move beyond the first two stages, and struggle to make a Decision. In high performing teams there is a continuous and easy flow though the OODA loop. The organisation is open to new information, makes sense of it, converts that situational awareness into a Decision, and can act on those decisions.

Reflection

- How effectively does the team you lead move through the OODA loop?
- Are there any areas in the model where you tend to get stuck?

3.6 Building a Great Team – From Stagnation to Excellence

Effective leaders engage others in pursuit of a Clear and Compelling Purpose. In other words, leaders have their impact in the world through the effective and high performing teams they create. Team building and empowering others is a fundamental aspect of leadership. Without an effective team, you will find you are incredibly busy, carrying a lot of responsibility and stress and not having much impact.

An effective framework for team performance development is Tuckman's 'Form to Perform' model[28]. I have adapted this to include my own observations, and to better link it to some of the ideas in this book. My version of the model is called 'Stagnation to Excellence' and it includes a focus on Clear and Compelling Purpose, building a Mission Command Culture, and communicating at a high level; all concepts which you will find covered in this book. I use this model a lot. I am so passionate about it that I get teased by other leadership and team development nerds. But it is simple, easy to understand, and gives a roadmap for improvement.

Teams seldom develop themselves, and a common misunderstanding is that they will naturally progress from left to right through each of these stages in their life cycle. This is not true; most teams get stuck in Stagnate and never leave. It takes leadership and a little courage to move a team to Excel, and perseverance to keep it there. There is a natural gravitational pull that draws teams to Stagnate. This model shows you the cultural roadmap to excellence but, as a leader, you will need to get the engine started and navigate the journey.

Four Stages of Team Development

Stagnate	Rebel	Recontract	Excel
· Bureaucratic	· Issues exposed	· Define clear and compelling purpose	· Energised and creative
· Hierarchical	· Frustrations surface	· Focus on culture, atmosphere and values	· Excited by clear and compelling purpose
· Process more important than purpose	· Process challenged	· Understand freedoms and constraints	· High levels of trust
· Slow decision making	· Friction	· Agree process for effective decision making	· Mutual support
· Avoidance of responsibility	· Insecurity	· Match people to tasks	· Inclusive
· Internal competition	· Confrontation	· Focus on training and development	· Open and honest communications
· Issues avoided	· Resistance to change		· Freedom within boundaries
· Status conscious			
· Blame culture			
· Low level communications			
· Expectations met			
· Feels 'safe'			

Fig 16. Model showing the Four Stages of Team Development based on a model by Bruce Truckman, 1964.

There are 4 stages in this model, Stagnate, Rebel, Re-Contract and Excel.

Stagnate

In this stage, bureaucracy, status, and hierarchy matter. Doing things 'the right way' is more important than getting things done. This is the triumph of Process over Purpose. Decision making is slow, with a complex drumbeat of meetings and layers of leadership. Throughout the organisation people prefer to avoid responsibility. There is internal competition and suspicion between people, and between departments. Most of the tension bubbles away beneath the surface, in unspoken rivalries and internal competition. The fridge in this organisation is likely to be plastered in passive-aggressive sticky notes addressing the theft of milk. Tension is only expressed in private conversations, or at home, where partners are subjected to a full account of everything that is wrong at work. This is not a happy place: people here count down the days to holiday or retirement, and political sharks thrive.

However, superficially, things feel safe and expectations are met. No more than expectations are met, but people tend to follow the rules and do exactly what they are told to do. This sort of organisation runs okay; it lacks everything which you find in Excel, but it is just good enough to get by, so people there tend to bide their time, whilst quietly looking at adverts for other jobs.

Rebel

If Stagnate is a form of organisational constipation, Rebel is the laxative which gets things moving, but not necessarily in a good way. As the name suggests Rebel can be a bit wild and a bit scary.

Rebel is usually cued by a change, often a new leader, or a change in circumstances that applies pressure to the organisation. In Rebel, people start exposing issues, demanding better and challenging the process. The result is usually friction, a feeling of insecurity, confrontation, and resistance to change. Rebel is an uncomfortable place.

A lot of leaders and teams will lose their nerve and retreat to Stagnate. People prefer the dull certainty of Stagnate to the risk of trying to move through Rebel. An effective leader will minimise the time that a team spends in Rebel by moving swiftly to Recontract. People sometimes ask if it is possible to skip Rebel; I can't reference my answer, but in my experience the answer is no, I have never seen a team develop without going through this stage, but skilful leaders will move through to Recontract quickly. It usually requires a certain amount of moral courage to lead a team through this phase; it can be an exhausting environment for a leader. Having a strong sense of purpose will help, and coaching or mentoring relationships can also be useful to the leader in this situation. Leadership in Rebel can feel lonely.

Recontract

Here the team works out and agrees the fundamentals of what they are about, what they are trying to achieve and how they are going to work. They are setting out the structure for success. In this stage, a team defines the Clear and Compelling Purpose and creates and nurtures the right culture. They agree freedoms and constraints, decide on a way of quick and effective decision-making, ensuring the right people are in the right roles and have the right training. Often, this is a case of going back to basics and getting the foundations right.

It is easy for people and organisations and teams to think they are too busy for this; routine process usually distracts people from this essential groundwork. But Recontracting is essential to set the conditions for high-performance, and regularly stepping back to check that you have these basics right is an important way of preventing the organisation sliding back into the shallow end of the performance pool.

Excel

This is what at you are aiming for when you are building a team. You will find that when most people are asked what sort of team they would like to be in, or to describe a successful team they have been in, this is what they describe. A team in Excel works in an energised and creative environment, where people are united and excited by a Clear and Compelling Purpose. There are high levels of trust and mutual support within the organisation. People feel included and they communicate openly and honestly; they are happy to talk about their emotions and feelings and express their opinions. In this sort of team there is the freedom to pursue ideas and projects, within agreed limits and as long as they clearly contribute to the overall purpose.

However, unless you work hard, your team is very unlikely to achieve Excel and will most certainly be stuck in the underachieving and turgid world of Stagnate.

The Fear and Performance Lines

On the model, I have shown a thick line that represents the fear barrier, which a leader and team must cross to move beyond Stagnate, and the performance curve which they will experience as they move from Stagnate to Excel. Performance is likely to drop in Rebel, stabilise in Recontract, and will then exceed the previous level when you reach Excel.

Four Stages of Team Development

Stagnate
- Bureaucratic
- Hierarchical
- Process more important than purpose
- Slow decision making
- Avoidance of responsibility
- Internal competition
- Issues avoided
- Status conscious
- Blame culture
- Low level communications
- Expectations met
- Feels 'safe'

Fear Barrier

Rebel
- Issues exposed
- Frustrations surface
- Process challenged
- Friction
- Insecurity
- Confrontation
- Resistance to change

Recontract
- Define clear and compelling purpose
- Focus on culture, atmosphere and values
- Understand freedoms and constraints
- Agree process for effective decision making
- Match people to tasks
- Focus on training and development

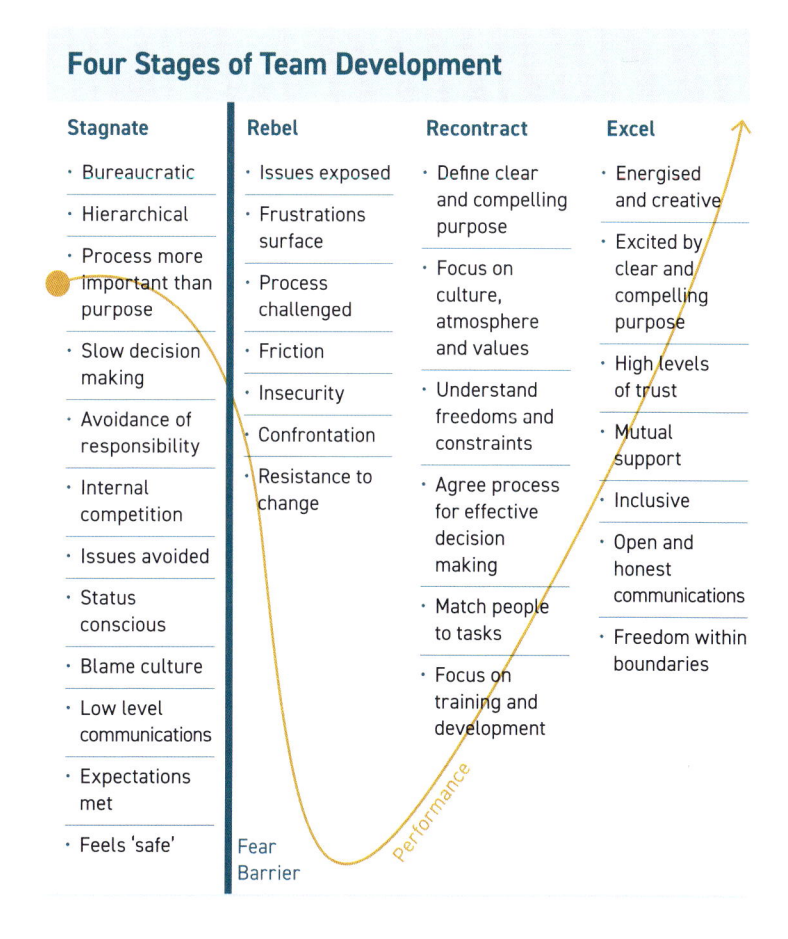

Excel
- Energised and creative
- Excited by clear and compelling purpose
- High levels of trust
- Mutual support
- Inclusive
- Open and honest communications
- Freedom within boundaries

Fig 17. Image showing fear barrier and performance line on the Four Stages of Team Development model.

Exercise

If you lead a team, explain this model to them and ask them where they would place themselves on this model. Then, as a team, discuss the results and consider what actions you can take to move towards or remain in Excel.

3.7 Reducing Friction – The Team Routine Service

The Team Routine Service is a concept you can try which will stop your team drifting into Stagnate. It is a simple idea which helps encourage continuous improvement and keeps relationships in the team healthy and positive. The idea is simple: stop what you are doing and look at how you are working as a team. This is very deliberately a question about how the team works and what results you are achieving.

An 'old banger' might pass you in the fast lane of the motorway with smoke billowing out of the exhaust. The car is meeting the objective of travelling fast, but the effort is unsustainable. In a poorly maintained team, goals and objectives are met, but underneath the surface there is friction and getting things done is harder than it needs to be. For a car to run well, it needs regular maintenance, and the same is true of teams.

Regularly, perhaps once a month or more, it is useful to bring the team together for a 'routine service' before parts of the engine start to break. This is how I suggest you do that:

Get the Atmosphere Right

It is important that the atmosphere is considered and a suitable place is chosen. I would suggest a neutral space, rather than the boss's office, and decent coffee or cold drinks should be provided. If you really want people to talk openly and honestly, it helps if they feel comfortable and valued.

Agree the rules

Before you begin, you should agree a few basics. Explain that you are actively looking for the team to continuously improve, and all ideas are welcome. You really must invite honesty and create an atmosphere where there is no threat of repercussions for saying the wrong thing. A useful rule in this process is that nobody in the room should DJE – Defend, Justify and Explain. Instead, encourage everyone to focus on being open to learning and developing.

Focus on a Question

Focus the team on a simple and open question such as: 'how could we work better as a team?' or 'how we can improve?' These questions invite people to look for improvements and positive change, which is far more useful than spending ages on what is wrong. Having asked the question, give people time to write down their thoughts in a notebook then invite feedback, but do so gently and if there is status in the room, think about reversing it so the most junior people speak first.

The process will work well if you make it a regular feature of the way that you operate, and if you make a point of acting on the ideas and suggestions that come out of the session.

Part Three **Leading Teams and Organisations**

"*The great enemy of communication, we find, is the illusion of it*".

William H. Whyte [29]

3.8 Getting Your Message Though - Barriers to Communication

Being able to communicate effectively is an important skill for leaders and organisations. As well as being able to connect with people by communicating at the right level on the Communications Pyramid (See Chapter 2.9), it is also useful to understand the various obstacles that stop a message getting through. If you understand the steps that a message must climb to have the desired effect, you can think carefully about how you communicate.

The model I use to explain this concept is one that was created by several friends of mine at the Leadership Trust, including Jon Davidge who I worked with for many years and who is without doubt one of the best leadership development consultants and facilitators in the UK. The model, (which I have adapted slightly), shows a series of steps, each of which must be successfully taken for a message to be effective. If it fails at any of these steps, then it will be ineffective. When you understand this model, you will understand why what was directed by one person, is not always what was done by the other. Successful communications are well-crafted and well-aimed.

The steps that a successful communication has to climb are:

Fig 18. Model inspired by Jon Davidge, John White, and Len Cresswell showing the stages a message has to pass through.

Spoken

The communication must be expressed. Verbal is ideal, which is where communications are most effective and compelling, but it could mean written or texted. It is surprising how often messages get stuck at this first hurdle. Very often, people say things like 'she should have known' or, 'they must know what I think', but on reflection, the message was never articulated or spoken. The first stage of getting a message through is to express it.

Heard

The communication must be received – by the right person. That might mean heard, or it could mean that the email or text has been read. Again, the most effective way of making sure the right person receives the right message is to speak to them directly, so they can hear your emphasis and understand your emotion.

Understood

Next the message has to be understood. Clear and concise language matters at this stage. Often people overcommunicate and the important part of the message gets lost in the padding. Communications need to be exactly the right length; too short and they miss key information; too long and important points are lost in the volume of unnecessary words.

Believed

Next the message has to be believed. This relies on the existing relationship between the people who are communicating.

During WW2 the BBC was listened to throughout occupied Europe, because people trusted them to tell the truth. People will be less inclined to accept a message from a source they do not fully trust.

So as a leader, being honest and straightforward is important, because if people trust you, your messages will be more likely to get through successfully. If you are not trusted, then however clearly you express yourself, the successful passage of your message will be undermined at this stage.

Engage

Next, the recipient of the message must be moved to engage. The message needs to be interesting or urgent enough to trigger an intellectual or an emotional engagement. Very often we receive information, but it does not move us to think or act. The message does not engage us, so we do not engage with it.

Action

If the message reached the right person or people and was credible, clear and compelling it will be translated into action. When you look back on the steps it has had to climb to reach this point, you can see why so often communication fails.

Back-briefing

To increase the chances of a communication successfully translating to action, actively check the passage of a message up the steps of this model through to action. The way to do this, is once people have been given a message, ask them to think about it and then come back to you and explain their understanding of it.

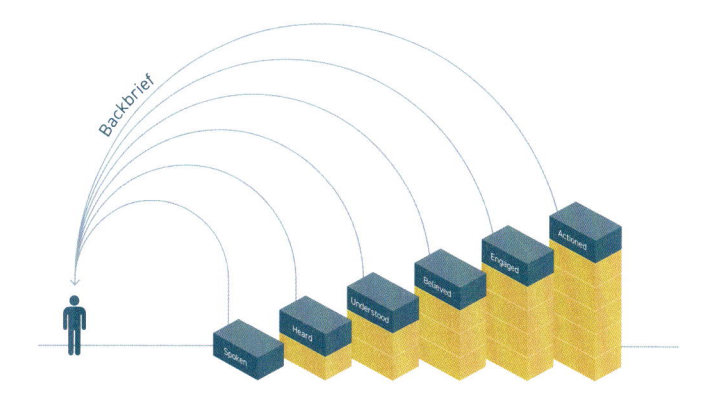

Fig 19. Backbriefing helps confirm the passage of a message.

Part Three **Leading Teams and Organisations**

You might also ask them how they feel about the message, so you can understand their engagement and commitment to whatever they are being asked to do. You might also ask them to confirm when they have acted on the communication. This technique is called back-briefing.

> **Back-briefing in Action**
> Back-briefing is used by leaders in the British Army. It is a convention that when a leader has received orders, the first thing they do is analyse those orders to make sure they make sense and that they understand them, and then they confirm their understanding back to the person that has issued them the orders. The person who has given the orders may then ask further questions to absolutely confirm understanding.

Reflection

With this model in mind, can you list up to three things you could do to communicate more effectively?

1 ....
2 ....
3 ....

3.9 PLC – 3 Components of Success

A few years ago, I was asked to run a session on team development at short notice for a local military headquarters in the North West of England. Given more time, I would probably have said too much and complicated the issue, but stood next to a whiteboard in a large and empty building that had at one stage been a stable for horses, I was forced to distil a lot of ideas into a simple model that I could explain in the 15 minutes I was allowed. The result is this very simple model I call the 3-Components of Success or PLC model.

I have chosen this to bring up the rear of the book because it is a very simple model which brings together many of the ideas and themes in this book. The three elements of PLC, which you will find in high-performing teams are: Purpose, Leadership and Culture.

Each of these components encourages and enables the growth of the other two. In an effective team you will find all three Components of Success. From time to time with an existing team, or when you are setting up a new team, it is worth scheduling some thinking and discussion time to make sure you have the right balance of these components. If all of these are right, the likelihood is that the organisation or team will be performing and running well.

Fig 20. An image showing the Three Components of Success

Purpose

I have already explained the importance of teams having a Clear and Compelling Purpose. Clear, so there is no misunderstanding and it is easy to understand and remember. Compelling, so that people are excited and engaged by it and want to move towards it. It is the role of the leader to define that purpose and to make sure that it is up to date and relevant. Where Purpose is not clear in a team or organisation, activity is not focussed. When that happens, different parts of the team or organisation often end up competing because they have different ideas about what they are trying to achieve.

Leadership

People throughout the team are allowed, and even expected, to have a leadership effect, increasing their own impact by engaging others intellectually and emotionally in pursuit of a Clear and Compelling Purpose. This is leadership based on personality and inspiration, rather than position and obligation. This sort of leadership is not hierarchical, it thrives at all levels in an effective team. People can lead in any direction to create positive action. Leadership throughout the team or organisation is tremendously energising and effective leadership translates into positive momentum.

Culture

The culture will be creative and energised. There will be an elevated level of trust and mutual understanding between people and departments; people will have considerable autonomy to make decisions and focus effort; and different parts of the organisation will support each other. People will feel excited about what they are working towards; they will feel part of the team and the wider organisation with an emotional rather than just professional, connection.

As you read my explanation of this model, you will see how it cements the ideas and themes that came before in this book. The importance of purpose, culture and connecting with people.

Leadership really is that simple, and the more you read, the more you will recognise that the basics are simple, consistent, and easily applied.

Reflection

Think about your own team or organisation. In relation to the PLC model, give yourself a score out of 10 for each of the 3 elements of the model. If the score is below 30, try to list some actions you could take to improve the score.

	Score / 10	**Improvement Ideas**
Purpose		
Leadership		
Culture		

PART FOUR

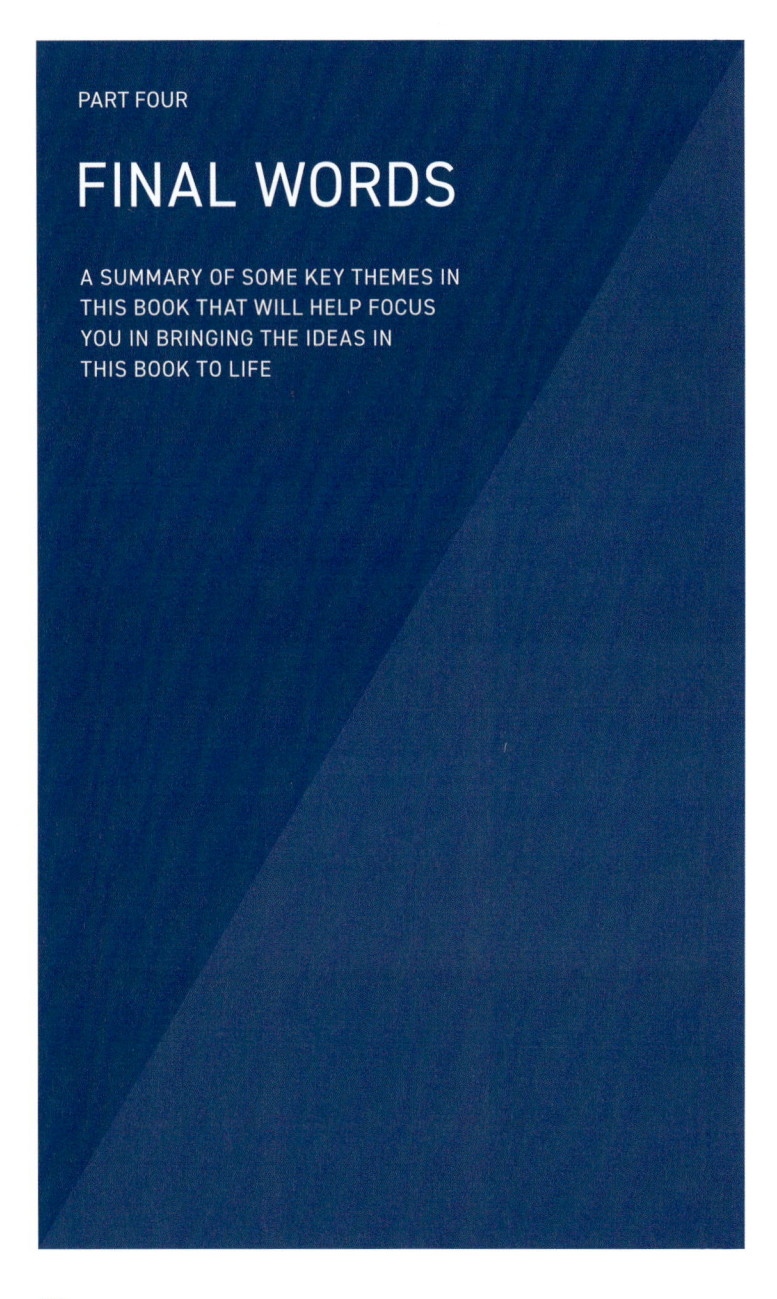

FINAL WORDS

A SUMMARY OF SOME KEY THEMES IN THIS BOOK THAT WILL HELP FOCUS YOU IN BRINGING THE IDEAS IN THIS BOOK TO LIFE

I hope you have found the book both interesting and useful. If you have read this far, then it was interesting; if it makes you a more effective leader, then it was useful. In this last section, I have captured a few ideas which I hope will help you to focus on a few core concepts.

Some thoughts on leadership

- Honesty is an essential characteristic of an effective leader.
- Some people wield their authority heavily; they dominate, intimidate, and manipulate. This sort of leader is to leadership as Voldemort is to magic.
- Leaders are at their best when they are healthy and happy. Take time to exercise, rest and think.
- Being clear what you are trying to achieve is essential. To create a clear, unambiguous objective is a key part of unifying the energy of a team.
- Leadership flows from personal power rather than positional power. It is always possible to lead kindly, even when tough decisions must be made.
- Building positive relationships is a core leadership activity.
- Allow small failures and use them as the basis for learning and development.
- If you are micro-managing, you are doing somebody else's job instead of your own. Build a team that you trust, and then give them freedom within boundaries.
- The leader does not need to be the cleverest or most knowledgeable person in the team. The leader just needs to be able to harness the cleverest and the most knowledgeable people.
- Keep plans as simple as reasonably possible. The more complex a plan, the more likely it is to go wrong. A key part of leadership is absorbing complexity.

I wish you the best of luck in whatever it is you seek to lead or change in the world. I hope that the ideas, models, and underlying principles in this book will support you in your work. The world needs positive and competent leadership now more than ever. I hope that in a small way this book contributes to that end.

End Notes

1. Jurd, N., 2020. Neil Jurd Developing Leaders. [LinkedIn] 28/10/2020. Available from: www.linkedin.com/in/neiljurd/ [Accessed 28 Oct 2020].

2. PNBHS.School.NZ, 2003. Address by field marshal the viscount slim on 14 October 1952 to officer cadets of the royal military academy Sandhurst. [Website] Available at: www.pnbhs.school.nz/wp-content/uploads/2015/11/Slim.pdf * [Accessed 28 Oct 2020].

3. Weber, M., 2015. Bureaucracy. In Working in America (pp. 29-34). Routledge.

4. Von Clausewitz, C., 1873. On war (Vol. 1). London, N. Trübner & Company. Von Clausewitz, C., 1956. On war (Vol. 2). Jazzybee Verlag.

5. Lewis, C.S., 1946. Man Or Rabbit? Student Christian Movement in Schools.

6. Smyth, J.G. and Smyth, J., 1961. Sandhurst: The History of the Royal Military Academy, Woolwich, the Royal Military College, Sandhurst, and the Royal Military Academy Sandhurst, 1741-1961. London: Weidenfeld & Nicolson.

7. Marine Corps Leadership Principles and Traits https://theleadershippodcast.com/wp-content/uploads/2016/08/Leadership-Principles-and-Traits.pdf (Accessed 10 Sept 20)

8. Centre for Creative Leadership, 2020. What are the characteristics of a good leader? [Online Blog] Available at: www.ccl.org/blog/characteristics-good-leader/* [10/06/2020].

9. Clayton, P., 2012. Octavia Hill: social reformer and co-founder of the National Trust. Pitkin Pub.

10. The Military Leader, 2014. The Military Leader. Grow yourself. Grow your team. [Website] Available at: https://themilitaryleader.com/quotes/quote-rommel-example-2/ * [Accessed 20 Oct 2020].Leader. Grow yourself. Grow your team. [Website] Available at: https://themilitaryleader.com/quotes/quote-rommel-example-2/ * [Accessed 20 Oct 2020].

11. The Editors of Encyclopaedia Britannica, 2020 Available at: https://www.britannica.com/science/Newtons-laws-of-motion (Accessed 20 Aug 20)

12. Merrill, D.W. and Reid, R.H., 1981. Personal styles & effective performance. CRC Press.

13. Syrus, P. and Lyman, D., 2015. The Moral Sayings of Publius Syrus: A Roman Slave. Lulu. com

14. Good Reads, 2020. Aristotle Quotes. Knowing yourself is the beginning of all wisdom. https://www.goodreads.com/quotes/3102-knowing-yourself-is-the-beginning-of-all-wisdom Available at: * [Accessed 10 Oct 2020].

15. Myers, I.B., 1962. The Myers-Briggs Type Indicator: Manual (1962).

16. Cattell, H.E. and Mead, A.D., 2008. The Sixteen Personality Factor Questionnaire (16PF).

17. Good Reads, 2020. Ronald Reagan. The greatest leader. Available at: at https://www.goodreads.com/quotes/123481-the-greatest-leader-is-not-necessarily-the-one-who-does * [Accessed 18 Sept 2020].

18. Powell, J., 1999. Why am I afraid to tell you who I am?. Zondervan.

19. The Editors of Encyclopaedia Britannica, 2020. Sir Henry Montgomery Lawrence. Available at: https://www.britannica.com/biography/Henry-Montgomery-Lawrence [Accessed 10 Sept 2020].

20. Jurd, N. Template for a Developmental Conversation. Published on Linkedin 28 Oct 2020. Available at: https://www.linkedin.com/feed/update/urn:li:activity:6727191145362919424/

21. Gallwey, W.T., 2001. The inner game of work: focus, learning, pleasure, and mobility in the workplace. Random House.

22. Jurd, N., 2020. Understanding Yourself –Input, Process and Output. [LinkedIn] 28/10/2020. Available from: https://www.linkedin.com/in/neiljurd/ [28 Oct 2020].

23. Jurd, N., 2018. Firm foundations. Available at: https://neiljurd.com/2011/08/firm-foundations

24. For a deeper understanding of this subject, the British Military Doctrine of Mission Command can be found at: https://assets.publishing.service.gov.uk/government/uploads/system/uploads/attachment_data/file/605298/Army_Field_Manual__AFM__A5_Master_ADP_Interactive_Gov_Web.pdf

25. See PBS Video available at: www.pbs.org/video/frontline-class-divided

26. Boyd, J.R., 1987. Organic design for command and control. A discourse on winning and losing.

27. Napoleon. I cannot find a robust source for this quote, although it is widely repeated on website. See: www.quotes.net/quote/42743 (Accessed 28 Oct 20)

28. Tuckman, B.W. and Jensen, M.A.C., 1977. Stages of small-group development revisited. Group & Organization Studies, 2(4), pp.419-427.

29. William H Whyte. 1950 September, Fortune, "Is Anybody Listening?" by William Hollingsworth Whyte, Page 174, Published by Time, Inc., New York. A version of this quote is usually incorrectly attributed to George Bernard Shaw. See https://quoteinvestigator.com/2014/08/31/illusion/#note-9667-1

Neil Jurd has produced a series of videos about leadership, which include many of the ideas in this book

The average video length is 8 minutes, and they are brought to life with simple graphics. If you would like to know more about these videos, please go to Neil's website, neiljurd.com

If you would like to talk about accessing these videos for team or organisational development, please contact sales@neiljurd.com or you can scan this code...

If you would like Neil or a member of the Neil Jurd Leadership and Team Development team to work with your organisation or to speak at an event, please email sales@neiljurd.com or make contact through neiljurd.com

Neil brings his passion for leader development together in this excellent book that you can keep referring to for inspiration and to help with personal reflection on leadership.

Brigadier Stuart Williams OBE

This excellent book provides succinct but coherent guidance on leadership.

Dr Maria Kontogianni, Principal Lecturer in Psychology, Nottingham Trent University

A hugely practical and easy to use handbook for leaders everywhere.

James Batchelor, CEO Alertacall

A fantastic guide and a must read for anyone involved in leadership and team development.

Steve Hill MBE

Neil is an inspiring world class leader who has dedicated his life to helping others learn, grow and develop.

Jordan Wylie, Author and Adventurer

Simply, Neil is the leading authority on Leadership. Coming from a man who walks the talk, this clear and concisely written book is a must for anyone in a leadership position wishing to positively enhance their own development or that of their team.

Craig Mathieson, Founder Polar Academy

Thank You

I have been helped and supported hugely in bringing this book together by quite a few people, and I would like to offer them my thanks. My daughters Matilda and Elsa, for allowing me long hours at my desk, and for many years accepting me going away to run courses and learn the business of leadership. Macarena Vergara, for her love and wisdom. To Glyn and Dan, who have both encouraged me to 'go large' with my ideas. Neither actually used the phrase 'go large'. James Batchelor, who told me to write a book and produce video content a long time ago, and now actually says 'I told you so' whenever we discuss these things. Gresty, the graphic designer who turned my scribbles into something presentable. Vanessa Dawkins, for helping me with the original graphics, Frankie Crowhurst, for her support, Dr Maria Kontogianni for helping with referencing. Then, in the final stages, Major Andy Thackway, Lt Col Paul Vickerman and Dr Jonathan Colman for their proof-reading. I am fortunate to have such good friends.

Notes

The Leadership Book by Neil Jurd

Notes

Notes

The Leadership Book by Neil Jurd

Notes